Praise for *The Il*

"No one should be allowed near a _____ of a keyboard until they have read this book. It is an antidote to the tediously direct and transactional nature of much of modern marketing."
—*Rory Sutherland, author of* Alchemy, *vice-chairman of Ogilvy*

"This book will make you better at your job. If you're trying to get your head around behavioural science, or how to apply it, look no further – Shotton has done all the hard work for you. Keep a copy within arm's reach – you'll be coming back to it time and again."
—*Jonah Berger, marketing professor at the Wharton School at the University of Pennsylvania and internationally bestselling author of* Contagious

"People behave in surprising ways, often driven by cognitive biases. *The Illusion of Choice* is a straightforward and practical guide to these biases and how to apply them. An essential read for every marketing professional."
—*Matthew Syed, Olympian and author of* Black Box Thinking

"Some books are designed to be impressive, written in complicated jargon. This book is designed to be useful, surprising, and practical, which is why it's written in plain English. Those other books look good on the bookshelf or behind your head on Zoom calls. This book you'll actually use."
—*Dave Trott, creative director, columnist at* Campaign *and multiple agency founder*

"Richard's approach to the world and to consumers is both radically different and incredibly scientific. Marketing is usually more about magic than science, but Richard shows us where to find the science and how to apply it to improve every element of our business. His first book, *The Choice Factory*, is one of my all-time favourites, and *The Illusion of Choice* is just as good. If you really want to understand your customers then this book is a must."
—*James Watt, founder of Britain's largest craft brewery, BrewDog*

"*The Illusion of Choice* explains lesser-known research in an easy-to-read manner to give consumers and businesses insights into how products persuade."
—*Nir Eyal, author of* Hooked: How to Build Habit-Forming Products

"*The Illusion of Choice* is provocative and practical. Shotton utilises the best of behavioural science to demonstrate surprising ways you can improve your business."
—*Seth Stephens-Davidowitz,* NY Times
bestselling author of Everybody Lies

"A short guide to applying behavioural economics to marketing, this book is both fun and useful. A great little bag of tricks!"
—*Les Binet, group head of effectiveness, adam&eveDDB*

"I learnt a ton through reading this book and enjoyed myself enormously in the process. Compelling, robust and eminently practical, *The Illusion of Choice* is a powerful guide to the psychological dynamics shaping behaviours in a complex world."
—*Nathalie Nahai, author of* Webs of Influence

"People talk about the 'difficult second album syndrome'. Not here. Richard's done it again."
—*Phil Barden, author of* Decoded: The Science Behind Why We Buy

"Richard has written a smart, enjoyable and extremely practical book around the unconscious biases and motivations which guide our everyday decisions in business and beyond. Told through a clever 'day in the life' device, academic experiments and real-world stories are shared, which draw the reader in enabling real insight and understanding. I would not hesitate to recommend *The Illusion of Choice* to anyone who wants to understand human behaviour and then apply that to business decisions. This is a book that would be equally useful for a global CEO or CMO or a bootstrapping start-up or scale-up leadership team."
—*Amelia Torode, former CSO of TBWA and
founder of the Fawnbrake Collective*

Praise for *The Choice Factory*

"This book is a Haynes Manual for understanding consumer behaviour. You should buy a copy – and then buy another copy to give to one of the 97% of people in marketing who are too young to remember what a bloody Haynes Manual is."

—*Rory Sutherland, columnist for* The Spectator
and executive creative director, Ogilvy One

"In a cacophony of overstatement, Richard Shotton possesses a melodious and balanced voice. In this short but powerful tome you can learn about how marketing actually does influence consumers. Or, for the more prosaic among us, how to get people to re-use towels, buy wine when German Oompah music is playing and select a broadband supplier by mentioning Charing Cross Station. The book also mentions me (all too briefly) which I also find enticing."

—*Mark Ritson, columnist for* Marketing Week
and professor at Melbourne Business School

"Actionable, memorable and powerful... Shotton has taken the jewels of behavioural economics and made them practical."

—*Seth Godin, author of* All Marketers Are Liars

"Comprehensive, compelling and immensely practical, *The Choice Factory* brings the building blocks of behaviour change together in one place."

—*Richard Huntington, chairman and chief
strategy officer, Saatchi & Saatchi*

"A top-class guide for those who want to put BE to work, rather than just illuminate their journey to work."

—*Mark Earls, author of* Herd

"A guide to your own mind, a roadmap of your blind spots, a toolkit for better advertising. *The Choice Factory* employs robust behavioural science in an approachable manner to demonstrate how you make and influence decisions. Synthesizing a vast body of research, live

experiments and numerous examples, Richard Shotton shows that there is a bias for every occasion and how to use them as tools to craft better communications."
—*Faris Yakob, author of* Paid Attention

"Richard delivers a wealth of cases proving the efficacy of working with, rather than against, the grain of human nature. This is catnip for the industry."
—*Phil Barden, author of* Decoded: The Science Behind Why We Buy

"Richard Shotton's application of behavioural economics is bang on the button. This book is timely, insightful, fascinating and entertaining."
—*Dominic Mills, former editor of* Campaign

"If you're a marketer, understanding what really makes people tick – as opposed to what they might tell you – is vital. This book takes us on an elegant, witty and digestible tour of the 25 main principles of behavioural science. Richard Shotton has read widely so that you don't have to, but he gives full credit to his many sources should you wish to pursue any of the topics further. This is a delightful and indispensable read for anyone in marketing, particularly those early in their careers."
—*Tess Alps, Chair of Thinkbox, the UK's marketing body for commercial broadcasters*

"At last someone has written a common-sense, practical guide to using behavioural science to sell things. It is backed by lots of research and working examples drawn from the author's own experience and his encyclopaedic knowledge of the industry. In short, this is a classic advertising textbook in the making."
—*Steve Harrison, British copywriter, creative director and author*

"This beautifully written book brings to life the counter-intuitive ways in which we make our everyday decisions."
—*Jules Goddard, fellow, London Business School.*

"*The Choice Factory* is a fun easy read packed with sound research that marketers can apply to their businesses immediately."
—*Nir Eyal, author of* Hooked: How to Build Habit-Forming Products

The
ILLUSION
of
CHOICE

Also by Richard Shotton

The Choice Factory

The
ILLUSION
of
CHOICE

**16½ PSYCHOLOGICAL BIASES
THAT INFLUENCE WHAT WE BUY**

Richard Shotton

HARRIMAN HOUSE LTD
3 Viceroy Court
Bedford Road
Petersfield
Hampshire
GU32 3LJ
GREAT BRITAIN
Tel: +44 (0)1730 233870

Email: enquiries@harriman-house.com
Website: harriman.house

Paperback ISBN: 978-0-85719-974-4
eBook ISBN: 978-0-85719-975-1

British Library Cataloguing in Publication Data
A CIP catalogue record for this book can be obtained from the British Library.

CONTENTS

INTRODUCTION

HAVE YOU EVER wondered why margarine is yellow? You might have assumed it was just a factor of the manufacturing process. But when margarine was invented, it had an off-white hue – uncharitable folk might even have said it was grey.

The change to the now-familiar colour came later and was primarily due to Louis Cheskin, a Ukrainian psychologist who had been hired by Good Luck margarine in the 1940s to boost their flagging sales.

To understand why shoppers picked butter over margarine, he set up an experiment. He invited local housewives to a series of lunchtime lectures. These talks were preceded by a buffet; nothing fancy – just triangles of white bread and chilled pats of butter.

After the talk finished, Cheskin chatted amiably with the attendees.

"How engaging was the lecture?"

"Did it last too long?"

"How well dressed was the speaker?"

"Oh, and one final question… what did you think of the food?"

Cheskin repeated this experiment half a dozen times, alternating between serving margarine and butter. The results fitted with the prevailing opinion of the two spreads: the diners made far more derogatory comments about margarine than butter.

But there was a twist.

In the tests, he'd dyed the margarine yellow and labelled it butter and dyed the butter white and labelled it margarine. When the participants were disparaging the margarine as oily, they were actually commenting on butter.

The purpose of Cheskin's charade was to prove that the enjoyment of margarine was determined by our expectations. All the elements of the experience – colour, smell, even the packaging – contributed to our expectations and therefore the taste. Cheskin called this phenomenon "sensation transference".

Cheskin used his theory to make suggestions to the marketing team at Good Luck. His most important recommendation was to change the colour of margarine from off-white to yellow, so it would benefit from buttery associations.

It wasn't just Good Luck who harnessed this tactic. Other brands swiftly copied the yellow colouring and category sales soared. In the 1950s margarine overtook butter in popularity – a lead it held for more than 50 years.

Good Luck's approach was once typical. Brands would regularly hire psychologists to understand what they could do to boost their sales. Cheskin alone worked with brands ranging from Betty Crocker to Marlboro, Gerber to McDonald's.

A subliminal challenge

However, the centrality of psychology to brands wasn't to last. In 1957 Vance Packard wrote a book called *The Hidden Persuaders*. It sold more than one million copies and caused a sensation.

In the book, Packard reported a series of revelations by a consultant called James Vicary into 'subliminal advertising'. This was a phrase that Vicary had coined to describe the practice of adding hidden messages to communications. These messages were supposedly flashed up for 1/3000th of a second – too quick to even be consciously noticed. Vicary claimed that he had run such a campaign in a cinema and boosted the sales of popcorn and Coke by nearly 70%.

In the fevered atmosphere of the Cold War, these tales of manipulative hidden messages sounded a bit too close to Orwellian mind control. The media whipped up a frenzy of condemnation and the American government banned subliminal ads. In the fallout, the use of psychological techniques in general was tarnished by association, and this body of insights fell out of fashion.

Tall tales of Big Brother

It later turned out that Vicary had invented the tale of subliminal advertising and that he never conducted any tests. But by that stage it was too late. For more than 50 years psychological techniques remained shunned.

However, that's changing. The benefits of applying behavioural science and psychology to marketing are so strong that it was only a matter of time before they returned. There are three compelling reasons – the three Rs – why you should be interested in this field.

First, *relevance*. It's hard to think of a subject more relevant to sales and marketing than behavioural science and psychology. Think about the key challenges any business faces: encouraging shoppers to switch from a competitor brand, to pay a premium or to buy a broader range of its items. These are all challenges of behaviour change. Businesses are in the business of behaviour change.

So why wouldn't you want to learn from 130 years of experimentation into what makes for effective behaviour change? That's all behavioural science is.

The relevance of the topic can be seen in Cheskin's study. He wasn't researching abstract academic concepts. His insight that expectations affected taste had practical applications. It meant that Good Luck margarine focused on changing the colour of the product rather than addressing taste directly.

Second, *robustness*. Some marketing theory has sketchy foundations. It's often based on intuition and gut feelings. That's not an ideal basis for multi-million-pound decisions.

Behavioural science is different. Nothing is taken on authority alone; everything has to be proved experimentally. Behavioural science is based on the peer-reviewed studies of world-renowned scientists. These solid foundations mean you can give the findings genuine credibility.

Again, think back to sensation transference. Cheskin didn't rely on a logical argument about the influence of looks on taste. Instead he set up a controlled study that analysed what actually affected taste ratings, rather than what people claimed.

Positive peer pressure

Fascinating as this study was, the robustness of behavioural science has improved since the 1940s. For example, Cheskin's study wasn't peer reviewed. Nowadays most findings are. There are certainly peer-reviewed studies on how expectations affect taste. For example, in 2006 Raj Raghunathan, a professor at McCombs School of Business, investigated the impact of perceived healthiness on taste.

Raghunathan invited a group of diners to sample a selection of Indian food and drink. Half of the guests were told that the lassi (a yoghurt drink) was healthy, while the other half were told that it was unhealthy. When the guests later rated the taste, those told the lassi was unhealthy scored it 55% higher than the others.

Finally, *range*. Behavioural science has its roots in social psychology, an academic subject which stretches back to the 1890s. Since then, psychologists have identified thousands of hidden drivers of human behaviour. This variety means that whatever brief you're tackling, there's likely to be a relevant bias that you can use.

Relevance, robustness and range are three strong reasons for applying behavioural science in your business. However, knowing you should apply behavioural science and actually applying behavioural science are different things.

When there is such a variety of biases, it can be hard to know where to start. This book aims to address that hurdle. Rather than race through a bewildering range of biases, I've selected the most pertinent: 16½ ideas that can both be applied easily and have the potential to make a large impact on marketing.

To make the ideas as easy to understand as possible we'll be following a single person through their day, looking at the choices they must make. Each chapter starts with a short outline detailing that decision. The rest of the chapter then looks at the behavioural science findings that are behind that thought process. For each of those findings we'll look at either existing academic findings or my own research and then, most importantly, how you can apply these findings to your commercial advantage.

Sound interesting? Well then, let's begin...

1

HABIT FORMATION

YOU'RE WOKEN BY the grating sound of your alarm. You get out of bed sluggishly and plod to the shower.

Now you've properly woken up, you get dressed and head to the kitchen.

After a quick cup of coffee and a slice of toast you're ready to leave. You shout "Bye!" to your partner and then you're out of the house on the way to the bus.

THINK ABOUT YOUR typical morning.

Even before you leave the house you have to make a succession of decisions: what to wear, what to eat, what route to take to work. The list goes on.

It's not just the morning. Every part of our life is filled with so many choices, from the trivial to the profound, that we tend not to weigh them all up in a considered manner. If we did, we'd never get through the day.

In the words of Princeton psychologist, Susan Fiske, we're "cognitive misers". Thinking is energy intensive, so we ration it.

Daniel Kahneman puts it rather more dramatically: "Thinking is to humans as swimming is to cats. We can do it but we'd rather not."

In order to limit how much we have to think, for many decisions, like what to buy, we often rely on habits – that is, we simply repeat what we did last time when faced with a similar situation.

Quantifying the importance of habits

The importance of habits has been quantified by Wendy Wood, a psychologist at the University of Southern California. In 2002 she recruited 209 participants and, every hour, as they were going about their day, prompted them with an alarm to write down what they were doing, where they were and what they were thinking about.

If someone was repeating the same action in the same place while thinking about something else, Wood characterised that behaviour as habitual. By her criterion, 43% of behaviour was habitual.

Since habits account for such a large proportion of behaviour, marketers need to understand the latest thinking on how to successfully create them.

Psychologists like B. J. Fogg, Nir Eyal and Wood have all created their own specific models describing habit formation. However, if we combine the findings from these models, there are six points that are relevant for business.

Let's run through each in turn.

How can you apply this bias?

1. Pick the right moment to break existing habits

Breaking an existing habit is hard. Perhaps the most memorable quote in this area comes from the Victorian author, Samuel Smiles. He wrote in his 1859 bestseller,[1] *Self-Help*:

> To uproot an old habit is sometimes a more painful thing, and vastly more difficult, than to wrench out a tooth.

This quote warns us that trying to disrupt a customer's existing habit indiscriminately is futile. It's best to pick a moment when habits are weakened.

Luckily for us, psychologists have identified several predictable moments when habits are weak. I covered some of these – such as nine-enders, life events and habits hardening over time – in *The Choice Factory*. But I missed out one of the most crucial moments: fresh starts.

The idea that people are most likely to adopt new behaviours at the beginning of new time periods – whether that's the start of a week, month, academic term or after a birthday – was first researched by Katherine Milkman of the Wharton School at the University of Pennsylvania.

She argues that people have a strong desire to be consistent. When we enter a new time period our relationship with our past self is weakened and it becomes a little bit easier to change our behaviour.

In 2014, Milkman ran a study alongside Hengchen Dai and Jason Riis. The study examined three behaviours:

---

[1] 'Bestseller' is a vague term which gets bandied about, but Smiles's book deserves the accolade. In the 50 years after publication, it sold 250,000 copies, outsold only by the Bible.

1. Dieting (through search volumes for relevant terms).

2. Gym usership (through university gym attendance).

3. Commitments to pursue new goals (through data from stickK, a website where people make public pledges to change their behaviour).

For all three data sets, the psychologists saw that new behaviours were much more likely to occur at the beginning of a new time period. For example, the probability of someone visiting the gym increased by 15% at the beginning of a month, 33% at the start of a week and 47% after a new term began.

The marketing implication is clear. If you want to disrupt a habit, target your messaging to the start of new time periods.

One example of this in practice comes from the West Midlands police. They recruited former offenders to write letters to prolific criminals, asking them to change their ways by enrolling in a police reform programme.

Sometimes the letters were timed to coincide with the criminal's birthday, a fresh start moment. On other occasions the message was sent at a random time. In a large-scale test of 2,077 letters there was a 4.1% response rate for the fresh start campaign, compared to 2.6% for the control. Even in an area as hard to change as crime, fresh starts can be effective.

A twist on Milkman's advice is to reframe an ordinary moment as a fresh start. In a 2015 study, Milkman and Dai recruited 165 students, each of whom had goals that they had been meaning to pursue. The researchers invited them to sign up for an email reminder to help them achieve these goals.

In some cases, the psychologists emphasised the date chosen for the reminders, 20 March, was a fresh start, by labelling it as the "first day of spring". In other cases, the same date was described more neutrally, as the "third Thursday in March".

The students were significantly more likely to sign up when the researchers drew attention to the fresh start. In that setting, 26% of students signed up, compared to only 7% when the date was described neutrally. Harnessing the fresh start effect led to a tripling of uptake.

This study suggests that those interested in behaviour change shouldn't just target new time periods with their messaging – they should also reframe seemingly mundane moments as fresh starts.

2. Don't rely on motivation – create a cue

Once you have disrupted an existing habit, your next task is to embed a new one.

One of the most robust findings is that if you want to encourage behaviour change, it's not enough just to boost motivation. Often, increased desire doesn't translate into behaviour change. In fact, that's such a common occurrence that psychologists have a term for it – the intention to action gap.

This is the idea that there is often a difference between what people intend to do and what they actually do.

Therefore, if you want to establish a habit you need to combine motivation with a cue: that is a time, place or mood that triggers the behaviour.

The importance of a cue has been demonstrated by Sarah Milne, a psychologist at the University of Bath. In 2002 she recruited 248 participants and randomly split them into three groups. The first group were told to record their exercise levels. When Milne met up with them a fortnight later only 35% had exercised for 20 minutes at least once a week.

The second group were also asked to record their exercise levels but, in addition, they read a motivational leaflet about the benefits of exercise. Two weeks later they met again with Milne. Even though the leaflet had boosted their intention to exercise, it barely changed their behaviour. A mere 38% exercised at least once a week. The intention to action gap again!

The third group were treated like the second group but, additionally, Milne asked them to state when, where and with whom they would exercise. Milne termed this an implementation-intention – in effect a trigger to remind them to exercise.

The motivation levels of this group were no different to the second group, but their behaviour was: 91% exercised at least once a week. The trigger gave the nebulous desire something to coalesce around.

If you want to create habitual purchasing behaviour, don't focus only on motivation. That's not enough. You also need to create a cue that will prompt that behaviour.

> Don't focus only on motivation. That's not enough. You also need to create a cue that will prompt that behaviour.

From lab to the real world

If you want a practical example of the power of cues, think of Pepsodent. When Claude Hopkins, the creative behind Pepsodent's ads, sought to improve dental hygiene in the US at the beginning of the 20th century, he didn't vaguely suggest tooth-brushing twice a day. Instead, the ads recommended brushing one's teeth after breakfast and before going to bed. A cue was at the heart of what was arguably the most successful public health campaign of the past 100 years.

The value of cues is still apparent today. A recent example comes from a 2019 savings campaign from Nationwide. The building society worked with ad agency VCCP to address the fact that 11 million people in the UK have less than £100 in savings. Rather than just focus on changing people's motivation to save, they also created a cue.

The cue they decided to use was payday. The slogan on the ads was *Pay Day = Save Day* and they ran lines such as "It's easier to save the day you're paid". These ads were upweighted to appear at the end of the month, when most people are paid.

True to their aim to change everyone's saving habits, not just their own customers', some of the posters ran outside competitor branches saying, "Make Pay Day your Save Day. Even if your savings account happens to be with these guys."

The campaign successfully boosted awareness – their tracking showed an eight-percentage point increase in agreement with the statement "Saving a little each month is important to do". It also changed behaviour; Nationwide finished the year with a net savings balance five times that forecast.

3. Use an existing behaviour
to create a cue

The Nationwide example points to another useful tactic. Rather than create a cue from thin air, it's often better to attach the behaviour you're trying to encourage to an existing cue. This is known as habit stacking.

In 2013, Gaby Judah from Imperial College London led a study among 50 participants into habit stacking. Half the participants were instructed to floss before brushing their teeth, whereas the remainder were instructed to floss afterwards. The order is important – an existing event acts as a better cue if it precedes the desired behaviour.

This was borne out in the results. The pre-brushing group flossed for 23.7 days, whereas the other group flossed for 25.2 days on average, a 6.3% improvement.

What type of cue should you use?

Not all cues are equally valuable. The more distinctive the better.

The evidence for this comes from another experiment by Katherine Milkman, this time working with Todd Rogers from Harvard University. In 2016 they approached 500 people outside a café and offered them a flyer with a $1 coupon off their next purchase the following Thursday.

Some of the people they approached were told: "When you see the cash register on Thursday, remember to use this coupon." This was the control group.

On other occasions, people were given the same cash register cue, but the flyer was also emblazoned with a stuffed green alien on the front and the words: "To remind you Thursday, this will be on the cash register." This was the test group.

On the following Thursday, the alien was placed by the cash register, where everyone could see it. It served as a reminder to use the coupon, but only for those in the test group who had been explicitly told to look out for the alien.

Of those who were instructed to look out for the stuffed alien, 24% redeemed their coupon, compared to just 17% of customers who received the control flyer.

If you want to change behaviour, it's best to make your cue as distinctive as possible.

4. Make the behaviour you're trying to encourage as easy as possible

The next step is the response – that's the behaviour you want to encourage. The best way to encourage a habit is to make it as easy as possible.

One way to make a behaviour easier is to use chunking. Split the behaviour into the smallest steps possible. In 2020, Milkman and her doctoral student, Aneesh Rai, conducted a study into the effects of chunking on goal completion.

Working with a charity, they asked new recruits to volunteer for a set amount of time across the first year. Some were asked to pledge 200 hours in their first year whereas others were asked to commit to four hours a week. The total is the same, but chunking the commitment led to an 8% improvement in volunteering levels.

This finding isn't a one-off. Shlomo Benartzi from the University of California led a study which found that it was more effective to ask people to save $5 every day, rather than $150 a month.

If a commitment appears bite-size, it looks less daunting, and people are keener to try it.

Chunking isn't the only way to make habits easier to embed. Contraceptive pills apply the principle of ease in a more lateral manner. The tablets only need to be taken on the first 21 days of a 28-day cycle to be effective. However, many birth control packets have 21 hormone pills, along with seven sugar pills. Pharmaceutical companies have realised that it's easier for people to maintain a habit if they take something every day rather constantly stopping and starting.

5. Harness the power of uncertain rewards

The next step is to create a reward. If a behaviour is to become embedded, people need to be rewarded – whether that's a psychological, physiological, or even a monetary reward. Of the six steps in habit creation, this is probably the broadest. But there's one underused area that marketers can effectively apply to their campaigns – the power of uncertain rewards.

The evidence for the power of uncertain rewards stretches all the way back to the work of B. F. Skinner. He was, according to the *Review of General Psychology*, the most influential psychologist of the 20th century. In 1930 he invented the Skinner box; a simple contraption that was nothing more than a wooden container with a lever inside, which dispensed pellets of food when the lever was pressed.

Skinner used the box to monitor all sorts of animals, from pigeons to rats. At first, the animals he placed in the box were oblivious to the lever. However, sooner or later, they'd bump into it and be surprised with a tasty treat.

This process of bump followed by reward would happen a few times until, eventually, the animals learned the function of the lever. From then on, as soon as they entered the box they'd head straight to the lever and begin pressing it repeatedly.

The psychologist used these rewards to train animals to complete increasingly sophisticated tasks. In one impressive demonstration of how far this technique could be pushed, his students taught a rabbit to pick up a dollar and deposit it through a slot in return for a treat.

Skinner dedicated his career to understanding what type of incentive most powerfully shaped behaviour.[2] One of his findings was that uncertain rewards were more influential than certain ones. When animals were only sometimes rewarded with food, the associated behaviour became more embedded than when they consistently received food.

It's a surprising finding, but one that we now know applies to people as well as rats and pigeons.

The human evidence for this comes from a 2014 experiment led by Luxi Shen, a psychologist at the University of Chicago. She recruited 87 participants and set them a challenge. Some participants

---

2   Not all of Skinner's studies were as successful as his eponymous box. He was also behind the slightly bizarre Project Pigeon: an attempt during World War II to train pigeons to guide missiles. Luckily for all our safety this project was scrapped when electronic guidance systems became more reliable.

were incentivised with a $2 reward (the certain condition), while others were offered a 50:50 chance of winning either $1 or $2 (the uncertain condition).

She found that when the reward was unpredictable, 70% of participants completed the task, compared to a mere 43% in the certain scenario.

Uncertain rewards are the answer to enhancing loyalty schemes

Even though the expected utility of the uncertain condition was lower, it was more motivating. The excitement of the uncertainty added a value beyond the monetary stake.

So, if you're trying to shape your customers' behaviour, harness uncertainty. If you have a loyalty scheme, stop offering every customer the same incentive each time they visit. Instead add a dash of randomness.

This is Pret's approach to boosting coffee sales. Unlike its competitors, it doesn't require its drinkers to collect reams of stamps in return for a free coffee. Instead, it empowers its staff to randomly reward customers with a free drink every so often.

Their tactic creates a far more positive reaction than the standard transactional approach. Here's the journalist Harry Wallop in *The Times* commenting on what it felt like to be given a free Pret coffee:

It was possibly the most powerful consumer loyalty programme in Britain. As a customer, you felt as if you'd won the lottery. I'd return to the office like a conquering hero and be applauded by colleagues for my stunning good fortune. God, I loved Pret.

But better still, consider Dishoom, the chain of restaurants based on Irani cafés in Bombay. At the end of a meal diners can roll a bronze dice, called the *Matka*. If they roll a six, then the meal is free.

It's mathematically equivalent to a 16.7% discount, but it feels wildly different on an emotional level.

6. Remember the three most important tactics: repetition, repetition, repetition

The final element of habit creation is the need for repetition. Habits aren't formed overnight. For a behaviour to become embedded you must repeat it.

A commonly quoted figure is that it takes 21 days to form a habit. But there's little meaningful evidence for this.

More robust data comes from Phillippa Lally at University College London. In 2009, she recruited 82 participants and asked them to start a new habit. These were simple behaviours, such as drinking a glass of water with lunch or doing a press-up after brushing their teeth.

On average it took 66 days until those behaviours were completed unthinkingly, which was Lally's definition of a habit. But that single figure masked sizeable variation – 95% of people formed a habit in somewhere between 18 and 254 days.

If you're trying to reshape behaviour, don't rely on a short burst of activity. You need more sustained interventions.

So, if you're trying to create habits remember the six key principles identified by behavioural science:

- Focus your efforts to break existing habits at the start of new time periods.
- Don't rely on motivating your audience to change. Motivation is a necessary but not sufficient condition. It needs to be combined with a cue or trigger.
- Rather than go to the effort of creating an entirely new cue it's often better to harness an existing behaviour.

- Make the behaviour you're trying to encourage as easy as possible.
- Harness the power of uncertain rewards.
- And finally, remember that habit creation requires a sustained series of interventions.

All these principles are important but the point about ease has applications far beyond habits. We'll be discussing the importance of making behaviour easy in more detail in the next chapter...

REFERENCES

'Habits in Everyday Life: Thought, Emotion, and Action' by Wendy Wood, Jeffrey Quinn and Deborah Kashy [*Journal of Personality and Social Psychology*, Vol. 83, No. 6, pp. 1281–1297, 2002]

'The Fresh Start Effect: Temporal Landmarks Motivate Aspirational Behaviour' by Hengchen Dai, Katherine Milkman and Jason Riis [*Management Science*, Vol. 60, No. 10, pp. 2563–2582, 2014]

'Put Your Imperfections behind You: Temporal Landmarks Spur Goal Initiation When They Signal New Beginnings' by Hengchen Dai, Katherine Milkman and Jason Riis [*Psychological Science*, Vol. 26, No. 12, pp. 1927–1936, 2015]

'Combining motivational and volitional interventions to promote exercise participation: Protection motivation theory and implementation intentions' by Sarah Milne, Sheina Orbell and Paschal Sheeran [*British Journal of Health Psychology*, Vol. 7, No. 2, pp. 163–184, 2002]

'Forming a flossing habit: An exploratory study of the psychological determinants of habit formation' by Gaby Judah, Benjamin Gardner and Robert Aunger [*British Journal of Health Psychology*, Vol. 18, No. 2, pp. 338–353, 2013]

'Reminders through Association' by Todd Rogers and Katherine Milkman [*Psychological Science*, Vol. 27, No. 7, pp. 973–86, 2016]

'The Benefits of Specificity and Flexibility on Goal-Directed Behaviour over Time' by Aneesh Rai, Marissa Sharif, Edward

Chang, Katherine Milkman and Angela Duckworth [*Working Paper*, 2020].

'Temporal Reframing and Participation in a Savings Program: A Field Experiment' by Hal Hershfield, Stephen Shu and Shlomo Benartzi [*Marketing Science*, Vol. 39, No. 6, pp.1033–1201, 2020]

'The 100 Most Eminent Psychologists of the 20th Century' by Steven Haggbloom, Renee Warnick, Jason Warnick, Vinessa Jones, Gary Yarbrough, Tenea Russell and Emmanuelle Monte [*Review of General Psychology*, Vol. 6, No. 2, pp. 139–152, 2002]

'The Motivating-Uncertainty Effect: Uncertainty Increases Resource Investment in the Process of Reward Pursuit' by Luxi Shen, Ayelet Fishbach and Christopher Hsee [*Journal of Consumer Research*, Vol. 41, No. 5, pp. 1301–1315, 2015]

'How are habits formed: Modeling habit formation in the real world' by Phillipa Lally, Cornelia van Jaarsveld, Henry Potts and Jane Wardle [*European Journal of Social Psychology*, Vol. 40, No. 6, pp. 998–1009, 2009]

2

MAKE IT EASY

LUCKILY THE BUS to the station isn't too busy and you get a seat. Or at least half a seat. The passenger next to you seems to be taking up far more than their fair share.

You try to distract yourself with some life admin. You haven't booked anywhere for your summer holiday yet and you're worried that the best places will sell out, so you start searching for a villa on a comparison site.

At first, it's rather enjoyable, imagining the fun you'll have on the trip. But there are so many interchangeable options. How can you pick from the seemingly endless array on offer?

It's just so difficult. Why can't they make it easier?

Frustrated with your wasted efforts, you give up and instead silently seethe at your neighbour.

TIM HARFORD, AUTHOR of *The Undercover Economist*, uses a simple analogy to describe behaviour change: you either press on the accelerator or you release the handbrake. Encourage motivating forces or remove restraining forces.

Marketing likes to pump the accelerator. It fixates on changing motivation above all else. But is this the right priority?

Evidence from Kurt Lewin – the German psychologist who Daniel Kahneman refers to as his "intellectual godfather" – suggests not.

Lewin, a professor at the University of Berlin in the 1930s, developed a set of ideas known as force field analysis. This theory describes behaviour as an equilibrium between two sets of forces – helping and hindering.

Lewin's insight was that people mistakenly fixate on helping forces when they should give precedence to hindering ones. Going back to Harford's car analogy, marketers should think more about releasing that handbrake rather than pushing on the accelerator. This change in priorities has practical implications.

> People mistakenly fixate on helping forces when they should give precedence to hindering ones. Think more about releasing the handbrake rather than pushing on the accelerator.

In Kahneman's words:

> Diminishing the restraining forces is a completely different kind of activity, because instead of asking, 'How can I get him or her to do it?' it starts with a question of, 'Why isn't she doing it already?' Very different question. 'Why not?' Then you go one by one systematically, and you ask, 'What can I do to make it easier for that person to move?' It turns out that the way to make things easier is almost always by controlling the individual's environment, broadly speaking.

More than anecdote

There's plenty of modern experimental evidence demonstrating the importance of removing obstructing forces.

For example, a 2017 study by Peter Bergman, from Columbia University, and Todd Rogers, from Harvard University, monitored the impact of friction on sign-up rates for a new educational service offering parents study tips for their children.

The psychologists randomly assigned parents to one of three sign-up routes. Each group received a text message telling them about the benefits of the service, but the sign-up mechanic varied in each group:

1. *Standard*: parents could enroll by visiting a website and filling in a short form.

2. *Simplified*: parents could sign up by replying 'Start'.

3. *Automatically enrolled*: parents were told that they were enrolled, but that they could opt out of the service by replying 'Stop'.

The sign-up rates varied according to the level of effort required: 1% for the standard group, 8% for the simplified group, and 97% for the automatically enrolled group.

Just as Lewin argued, small bits of friction – even in an important matter like our kids' education – have a disproportionate effect on our behaviour.

But that was just the first half of the experiment. Next, the psychologists recruited 130 teachers, told them about the experimental design and asked them to predict the sign-up rates in each scenario.

The teachers knew that friction would reduce sign-ups, but they wildly underestimated the scale. They predicted uptake of 39% for the standard group, 48% for the simplified group and 66% for the automatically enrolled group. They thought sign-up rates would vary by only 27 percentage points, whereas in reality, they differed by a whopping 96 points.

Let's look at how this effect can be applied in the real world.

How can you apply this bias?

1. Spend more time seeking out and eliminating friction

It is not just teachers who are prone to underestimating the importance of friction. It's a widespread issue and marketers are as culpable as any other profession. That's a problem. If we underestimate the impact of friction, we'll spend too little time and money simplifying our customer journey.

We need to put more effort into stripping out the smallest bits of friction, such as pre-populating forms, removing unnecessary steps, or encouraging irregular purchasers to become subscribers.

The impact can be immense. Think of Netflix and its switch to auto-playing the next episode. Or Amazon's introduction of one-click ordering.

Anything that reduces customer effort will have surprisingly large effects.

You may think that your product has as streamlined a process as possible. But it might be worth thinking again, as sometimes even the simplest of purchase journeys involves hidden friction.

Consider ordering a bottle of champagne in a fancy restaurant. What could be simpler than that? All you need to do is raise your arm and a waiter will glide over to take your order.

It sounds simple enough, but peer closer and you'll spot hidden barriers. For example, if you're with a friend, you'll have to break the flow of your conversation while you order. Or, if you're unlucky the waiter will be looking the wrong way and you'll be waving your arm around like a fool.

These are small inconveniences, but Kahneman's insight is that they will depress sales.

This is shown by the experience of the flamboyant Soho restaurant, Bob Bob Ricard. The restaurant, founded by ex-Ogilvy ad man Leonid Shutov, stripped out friction from champagne ordering by adding a 'Press for Champagne' button at every table. By eliminating the smallest of barriers, they released a great deal of pent-up demand – the restaurant sells more champagne than any other restaurant in Britain.

Even if you think you've streamlined your process as much as possible, remember the champagne button. Perhaps there's a similarly creative way of stripping out friction for your business.

Source: author's own image.

2. Focus on making the first step of the journey as easy as possible

Beyond the advice to look harder for pieces of friction, there are also some more counter-intuitive behavioural science techniques that can be applied. Let's start with one known as the foot-in-the-door technique.

In 1966, Stanford psychologists Jonathan Freedman and Scott Fraser visited homeowners in Palo Alto, California and gave them a short talk about road safety. The psychologists then asked the participants if they would erect a 'Drive Safely' sign in their front garden. The sign was large and, in the words of the psychologists "rather poorly lettered". Unsurprisingly, only 17% of the subjects agreed to the request.

A second group of homeowners was then approached. They received the same safety talk, but this time the psychologists made a smaller ask: that homeowners place a tiny sticker in their window supporting road safety. Virtually everyone agreed.

Two weeks later, the second group were revisited and asked if they would put up the large sign. Among those who had displayed the window sticker, 76% agreed.

Freedman and Fraser argued that a two-step approach is effective as it taps into people's strong desire to be consistent with their past behaviours.

In the words of the psychologists:

What may occur is a change in the person's feelings about getting involved or about taking action. Once he has agreed to a request, his attitude may change. He may become, in his own eyes, the kind of person who does this sort of thing, who agrees to requests made by strangers, who takes action on things he believes in, who cooperates with good causes.

If you want to encourage major behaviour change, begin by asking the audience to make a small change. It should be small enough that it takes minimal effort, but large enough to influence the self-identity of the target audience. Then, once they have made the minor change, follow up with your genuine ask.

3. Consider reducing the amount of choice you offer

Another slightly surprising way to make behaviour change easier is to reduce the amount of choice that you offer your customers. Evidence shows that offering too much choice can cause decision making to grind to a halt. Option overload can result in consumers choosing not to buy anything, or simply going for the default or cheapest option.

Evidence for what psychologists call choice paralysis comes from the work of Sheena Iyengar of Columbia University and Mark Lepper of Stanford University. In 2000 they set up a tasting booth at a posh supermarket, called Draeger's, in Menlo Park, California. Shoppers who passed the booth were offered the chance to sample a range of jams and they were given a $1 coupon to encourage them to buy.

On some occasions the stall had a limited selection of six jam flavours, on other occasions there were 24 varieties.

Of the 242 shoppers who passed the stall when it had an extensive selection, 60% (145) stopped and examined them further. This compared favourably with the limited range scenario, where only 40% of shoppers stopped (104 out of 260 passers-by).

However, what most marketers care about is not stopping rates, but purchasing. Here the story was different. In the 24-jam scenario only four people purchased (1.7% of all passers-by), compared to 31 in the six-jam scenario (12%). That's a seven-fold difference.

The psychologists argued that this experiment showed that "although having more choice might appear more desirable, it may sometimes have detrimental consequences for human motivations".

The implication seems obvious – reduce the choice that you offer your customer.

But before you rush to pare back your offering, it's worth considering follow-up research that suggests the genuine story is a little more nuanced. A 2015 meta-analysis by Alexander Chernev, a psychologist at Northwestern University, discovered that choice paralysis only occurs in some settings. In his analysis of 53 experiments, he identified four situations when people prefer fewer choices:

1. They have no well-defined preferences.

2. They are unfamiliar with the options.

3. The options are similar with no clear winner.

4. The options are difficult to evaluate, perhaps because they are presented poorly.

His research suggests that, if any of these factors apply to your category, then choice paralysis is a heightened risk. If not, your customer might be more accepting of plentiful choice.

4. Don't mess with your audience's worldview

So far, we have discussed literal ways to make behaviour change easier. These tend to focus on removing physical barriers.

But there are lateral applications too. And for these we should turn for inspiration to a campaign with household recognition in the US, but which is barely known in the UK. A campaign from the Texas Department of Transportation which aimed to reduce littering rates.

In the 1980s the Texans were grappling with the perennial problem of roadside litter, or 'trash', as they might say. Each year it cost $20 million to pick up the mountains of rubbish strewn along the roads. Each year the state ran ads asking the culprits to "Keep Texas Beautiful", and each year the litterers kept littering.

In 1985, frustrated by their lack of success, the Department hired the Austin ad agency GSD&M, led by the creative Tim McClure. McClure spotted that the previous ads had reflected the worldview of the clients – a committee, he jokingly said, with an average age of 107.

But the message of environmental stewardship fell flat with the wrongdoers – young, rule-breaking men. Or in his infamous words, "Bubbas in pick-up trucks".

McClure recognised that the barrier to behaviour change was a psychological one. The historic campaigns had tried to shift the worldview of the target audience. That's a sizeable hurdle; most people are loath to change their minds.

Instead, the agency altered the message to fit with the target audience's views. McClure created the slogan, "Don't Mess with Texas", which repositioned littering as an affront to state pride. It was something an interloper from Oklahoma might do, but certainly not something any true-blooded Texan would stomach.

It's arguably the most successful anti-littering campaign ever, reducing litter by 72% between 1987 and 1990. It was so successful that the phrase has entered popular culture – George W. Bush used it in his presidential acceptance speech and there's even an American nuclear submarine, the USS *Texas*, emblazoned with the motto.

We can apply behavioural biases literally by removing the physical barriers that prevent behaviour change. But the biggest benefits come when we apply biases laterally – removing the psychological barriers blocking change.

5. Add friction if you want
to reduce a behaviour

So far, we have discussed how removing barriers encourages desirable behaviour. But this idea can also be applied in reverse – if you're faced with an undesirable behaviour, then add friction.

A dramatic example can be seen in the field of suicide prevention. In September 1998, the British government introduced legislation to make paracetamol overdoses harder. From then on, shoppers were only allowed to buy one pack at a time and the maximum size of a pack was reduced (to 32 pills in a pack bought from a pharmacy and just 16 pills in generalist stores).

Even in a matter as serious as suicide, the addition of this tiny amount of friction had a beneficial impact. In 2013, Professor Keith Hawton, a director at the Centre for Suicide Research at the University of Oxford, undertook a study to understand the legislation's impact. After analysing mortality data (1993–2009, ONS) in England and Wales he estimated that there was a 43% reduction in deaths involving paracetamol after the legislation. That equates to an estimated 765 fewer deaths in the 11-year period he studied.

This topic of *making it easy* for our audience is instructive, because it challenges our fundamental assumptions about behaviour. We might assume that to change behaviour we must focus our efforts on underlying motivations. But if we do that, it means that we ignore the importance of ease in getting people to change their behaviour.

If we make the desired behaviour easier by removing barriers, or the undesirable behaviour harder by adding friction, we're more likely to get people to do what we want.

However, while that rule is true in most circumstances, there are rare occasions when a different tactic works best. Sometimes you should add friction to a desirable behaviour. If that sounds puzzling, don't worry, all will become clear in the next chapter...

REFERENCES

'Release the brake to combat climate change' by Tim Harford [*Financial Times*, 28 February 2020]

'How to Launch a Behavior-Change Revolution' [Ep. 306] by Stephen J. Dubner (with Daniel Kahneman)

'The Impact of Defaults on Technology Adoption, and Its Underappreciation by Policymakers' by Peter Bergman and Todd Rogers [*CESifo Working Paper Series*, No. 6721, 2017]

'Compliance without pressure: The foot-in-the-door technique' by Jonathan Freedman and Scott Fraser [*Journal of Personality and Social Psychology*, Vol. 4, No. 2, pp 195–202, 1966]

'When choice is demotivating: Can one desire too much of a good thing?' by Sheena Iyengar and Mark Lepper [*Journal of Personality and Social Psychology*, Vol. 79, No. 6, pp. 995–1006, 2000]

'Choice overload: A conceptual review and meta-analysis' by Alexander Chernev, Ulf Böckenholt and Joseph Goodman [*Journal of Consumer Psychology*, Vol. 26, No. 2, pp. 333–358, 2015]

Don't Mess with Texas: The Story Behind the Legend by Tim McClure and Roy Spence [2006]

'Long Term Effect of Reduced Pack Sizes of Paracetamol on Poisoning Deaths and Liver Transplant Activity in England and Wales: Interrupted Time Series Analyses' by Keith Hawton, Sue Simkin, Sue Dodd, Phil Pocock, David Gunnell and Navneet Kapur [*British Medical Journal*, Vol. 23, 2013]

3

MAKE IT DIFFICULT

AFTER A BUS journey that seemed twice as long as normal, you're finally at the right stop.

You get off and make your way to the train station. Your brisk walk is interrupted by a fundraiser, hunting for donations. The eager youth asks whether you could spare his children's charity a whopping £20 a week.

Outraged at the audacious sum, you turn him down. He back-pedals quickly, keen not to lose you.

Okay, he says, how about a pound a week? This seems reasonable, and you sign up, feeling pleased that you've made the world a slightly better place.

IN THE LAST chapter, we discussed Freedman and Fraser's foot-in-the-door technique. Their experiment demonstrated that making the first step on a journey as easy as possible boosts the probability of successful behaviour change.

But what would happen if you did the opposite? If you made the first step on the journey as difficult as possible? It might sound foolhardy, but it certainly worked for the charity worker in our example.

Rory Sutherland, the founder of ad agency Ogilvy Change, argues that sometimes behaving in the opposite way to that suggested by an experiment can be effective. He says:

While in physics the opposite of a good idea is generally a bad idea, in psychology the opposite of a good idea can be a very good idea indeed: both opposites often work.

But is Rory right?

The door-in-the-face technique

Luckily for us, we don't have to speculate. In 1975, Robert Cialdini from Arizona State University tested flipping the foot-in-the-door technique on its head. He called his new approach the door-in-the-face technique.

In his experiment, Cialdini approached people on a university campus and asked whether they would volunteer for two hours at the local youth detention centre. Less than 17% agreed.

Next, he approached a different sample of people with a more extreme appeal – would they volunteer for two hours a week for the next two years? It was such a preposterous request that everyone declined.

However, Cialdini didn't stop there with the second sample of people. He then made another request – the same one that he had previously asked the first group. Would they give up two hours of their time to help on a single afternoon? This time, 50% agreed.

People were almost three times more likely to comply if they had previously been asked to make a more sizeable commitment.

The impact extended beyond vague promises: actual attendance rates were also boosted. In the control condition, 50% of those who committed to help turned up. This figure rose to 85% when the door-in-the-face technique was harnessed.

But why does the door-in-the-face technique work?

One explanation is that it taps into a bias known as reciprocity. Reciprocity is defined by the sociologist Alvin Gouldner as the rule, present in all cultures, that, "You should give benefits to those who give you benefits." In his bestseller *Influence*, Cialdini lists reciprocity as one of the six most influential principles of persuasion. This assertion is supported by experimental data.

In 2007, Armin Falk at the University of Bonn sent out 9,846 genuine letters asking for donations to a charity working in developing countries.

Some of the potential donors received only a letter with information about the charity. Others received the same message alongside a gift: either a single postcard or a pack of four cards. Those who received the postcards were told they were a "gift from the children of Dhaka" that "can be kept or given to others".

When it came to responses to the letter, there was a marked difference in performance. Those who received gifts were significantly more likely to donate. Response rates rose by 17% for the single postcard and 75% for the larger gift.

Alongside an uplift in responses, there was also an increase in the size of donations. The average donation rose by 63p among those who had received a small gift and £3.65 if they had benefited from the larger gift of four postcards.

The link between reciprocity and the door-in-the-face technique

You might be thinking, how are reciprocity and the door-in-the-face technique linked?

Well, with the latter technique the requester opens with a big demand and then follows that up with a smaller one. In this two-step process the requester is making a concession. The principle of reciprocity suggests that the other party will feel a pressure to make a similar concession and agree to the smaller request.

In Cialdini's words, reciprocity means: "You should make concessions to those who make concessions to you."

Let's look at how to apply this effect practically.

How can you apply this bias?

1. Use a two-step approach to behaviour change

The door-in-the-face technique can be used in many commercial situations.

Think about a negotiation. The bias could be applied by opening with a sky-high price that you expect to be rebuffed, then when it is, following up with a more reasonable request. That second offer is more likely to be accepted than if you simply asked for it in one go.

Or consider trying to encourage someone to exercise. The door-in-the-face technique suggests you begin by encouraging budding athletes to complete a tough challenge, like committing to run a marathon. Then when that suggestion is turned down, follow up with something more achievable, like completing a 5km jog.

A contradiction between foot-in-the-door and door-in-the-face?

You may be wondering about whether the foot-in-the-door and door-in-the-face techniques contradict each other. How can they both be effective?

At first, this seems confusing. But maybe the contradiction is superficial. The techniques are both trying to achieve the same thing. They're both two-step approaches that try to make the first *genuine* step on the journey seem as easy as possible.

The foot-in-the-door technique does this by actually creating a really small initial action. The door-in-the-face technique is more lateral in its approach. There is never any intention that people would accept the opening offer. Its role is to make the first genuine step appear smaller in comparison.

> **With the door-in-the-face technique there is never any intention that people would accept the opening offer. Instead it makes the first *genuine* step appear smaller in comparison.**

The foot-in-the-door technique changes the actual size of the first step, whereas the door-in-the-facechanges the perceived size.

2. Apply the IKEA effect

Although the general theme of the last chapter was 'make it easy', there really are occasions when making the desired behaviour difficult has a value.

Evidence for this assertion comes from Michael Norton of Harvard University, Daniel Mochon from the University of California, and Dan Ariely from Duke University, and their 2012 paper, 'The IKEA Effect: When Labor Leads to Love'.

The paper opens with a striking anecdote. In the 1950s, more and more American women were entering the labour market, so increasingly households had both parents working. The General Mills brand, Betty Crocker, recognised that this trend would affect their home-baking business: busy working lives meant less time to make cakes from scratch.

Betty Crocker capitalised on this by launching an instant cake mix. Now, all a cook needed to do was buy the mix, add water, stir and pop it in the oven.

They sat back and waited for the sales. But despite astutely tapping into a social trend and creating a simple product, sales were disappointing.

Why was this?

At first, the management were stumped, but after a while they realised that they'd made the process too easy. After all, baking isn't just about getting calories on board quickly; often cakes express your love for a family member or friend. How much love can you really convey if that process is so easy?

So, Betty Crocker decided to complicate the baking process by adding an extra step – now cooks had to add an egg to the mix.

The simple act of requiring a little more effort made people feel they were more like proper cooks, and that was when sales began to take off.

From anecdote to evidence

It's a nice anecdote. But does it reflect a broader truth?

The academics decided to probe further. They recruited participants and asked half of them to assemble a plain black IKEA box. They called this group the builders. The other half, the non-builders, didn't have to make anything. Instead, they were shown a pre-assembled IKEA box.

Everyone was then asked to bid on their box and to rate on a seven-point scale how much they liked it.

On average the non-builders bid 48 cents for the box. In contrast, the builders offered 78 cents – that's an increase of 63%. Additionally, the builders liked the box 52% more than non-builders.

To check that the findings weren't a one-off, Norton, Mochon and Ariely repeated the experiment with origami birds rather than IKEA boxes. They saw consistent results.

The psychologists argued that we value things more if we have put some effort into getting them. They termed this, appropriately enough, the 'IKEA effect'.

If your concern is boosting a customer's evaluation of your product, then you might want to add in a bit of friction.

Adding friction

There are many ways to do this. In the world of food, Blue Dragon has leveraged this principle in their curry kits. By dividing the ingredients into separate units, the kits require more work on the part of the cook, boosting their appreciation of the end product.

Elsewhere, Apple has applied this principle to their packaging. According to Tom Vanderbilt, they spent months adding the right amount of friction to the opening process. They've created:

A box with the perfect drag and friction on opening to introduce an enticing pause as you unveil your new phone... The result is not just an elegant container but a carefully orchestrated ritual. You do not merely open this box as if you were tearing into a packet of crisps. You are welcomed inside.

Even wine can benefit. The effort of removing a cork can mean we appreciate what's inside more than when it comes out of a screw-top bottle.

If these examples feel a stretch, there's experimental evidence to back up the wine point.

In 2017, Charles Spence and Qian Wang from the University of Oxford recruited 140 participants and asked them to sample two Malbecs. On one occasion they drank the wine after opening a screw-top bottle, on another they were treated to a bottle with a cork.

Even though the participants unwittingly drank exactly the same wine, they rated the quality 10% higher and the taste 4% more intense when they had used a corkscrew to open the bottle.

With a clever follow-up experiment, the psychologists pinpointed that the boost to ratings came from the effort of opening rather than a general association of corks with quality. In their second study, people sampled two wines, but this time they didn't do the opening – they heard someone else do it. Some heard the pop of the cork being removed, others the noise of the screw cap. In this study, the boost to perceived quality fell to 8% and the boost to perceived flavour intensity to a mere 1%.

You have two separate tactics in 'make it easy' and 'make it difficult'. They can both have a positive effect on the brand. However, the nature of that boost varies. 'Make it easy' is the right tactic if you're prioritising action over attitude, whereas 'make it difficult' is appropriate if you want to improve quality perceptions.

You need to choose the right time to use each tactic.

3. Make sure your customers know the amount of effort you have gone to

If all this feels like an unpleasant trade-off, there are occasions when you can get the best of both worlds. Here we need to turn to an idea called 'the illusion of effort'.

Before we discuss the experimental evidence, let's turn to a story from Dan Ariely. The academic met an elderly locksmith at a concert who told him about his career. When the tradesman was a young apprentice, jobs would take him hours, and sometimes he'd have to resort to breaking the client's door. But he was well rewarded for his labours with generous tips.

Over the years, lock-picking had become quicker and easier for him. He'd get his customers inside in moments. But, instead of being rewarded for his expertise, his customers seemed to resent paying, let alone tipping!

The locksmith's tale demonstrates the illusion of effort. This is the finding that people tend to value things more when we see the work that has gone into them. So, rather than making it difficult for the end user, make sure they recognise how much effort and difficulty you as a brand have gone to.

This isn't supposition. There's academic evidence to back up this psychological bias.

In 2005 Andrea Morales, an assistant professor at the University of Southern California, tested whether consumers rewarded firms that demonstrate high effort.

In her study, participants read that they had hired an estate agent to help them find an apartment and that based on their preferences the agent created a list of ten recommended properties.

Participants believed the lists had been created in one of two ways. Half thought that the estate agent had spent nine hours creating the list manually; while half believed that the agent had only spent an hour and used a computer.

After reading the scenario, participants rated the agent from 1 to 100. In the low-effort condition, they rated the estate agent at 50 out of 100, whereas in the high-effort condition that figure rose to 68. That's a significant increase of 36%.

Show your efforts

Time and effort are not the only factors at play. Transparency is key: consumers need to be clear that work is going on.

The importance of transparency is demonstrated by a 2011 study by Harvard Business School researchers Ryan Buell and Michael

Norton. They asked 266 participants to use versions of a simulated travel website to book travel arrangements for a trip.

While the participants waited for the results, they were shown either a continually changing list of the flights being searched, or an opaque progress bar. Afterwards, they rated how much they valued the service.

The subjects rated the service 8% higher with increased transparency – that is when they could see the list of the flights being searched rather than the simple progress bar.

You need to make effort visible. You can do this literally, like the travel website example. Digital services are particularly amenable to this.

You can also do it with your PR. A great example comes from Dyson, they regularly promote the fact that they tested 5,127 prototypes in order to build the perfect vacuum cleaner.

Domino's has put the labour illusion to good use in-app with its operational transparency, where customers see a live feed of the tasks that go into making their pizza. Another example is the Spanish bank BBVA, which added an animation to its ATMs showing the notes being counted as customers wait for their cash.

There are opportunities for brands in the physical world too. Restaurants can harness this effect by letting diners see the hard work going on in the kitchens. In a separate experiment from 2017, Buell showed that if diners can see their food being prepared, they rate it 22% higher than the same food when they can't see it being prepared.

But be careful.

This bias doesn't justify a poor product. In a final experiment, Buell created a fake online dating site and manipulated the quality of profiles that users were matched with: sometimes they were shown suitable dates, sometimes unsuitable ones. He also varied whether he was transparent about the efforts the site was going to or not – on some occasions showing users how they were being matched up (by variables such as age, height, location, preferences), but on other occasions keeping this information hidden.

Buell's finding was clear. When the participants were shown a suitable match, the labour illusion made them even happier with the results. But when participants were shown an unsuitable date, being transparent about the effort made users even unhappier with the service. It seems this effect exaggerates people's opinions of brands rather than overturns them.

Make sure you harness this bias in your product design and marketing but, crucially, make sure that you have an admirable product in the first place.

In this chapter we've discussed a range of benefits to 'make it difficult'. However, there is one strength we haven't touched on yet. That's the idea that if you add in a little difficulty to the interpretation of a message, you can boost its memorability. It's a useful tactic for brands. So useful in fact that it deserves a chapter of its own...

REFERENCES

'Reciprocal Concessions Procedure for Inducing Compliance: The Door-in-the-Face Technique' by Robert Cialdini, Joyce Vincent, Stephen Lewis, Jose Catalan, Diane Wheeler and Betty Lee Darby [*Journal of Personality and Social Psychology*, Vol. 31, No. 2, pp. 206–215, 1975]

'Gift Exchange in the Field' by Armin Falk [Econometrica, Vol. 75, No. 5, pp. 1501–1511, 2007]

The IKEA Effect: When Labor Leads to Love' by Michael Norton, Daniel Mochon and Dan Ariely [*Journal of Consumer Psychology*, Vol. 22, No. 3, pp. 453–460, 2012]

'Zen and the art of opening an iPhone box' by Tom Vanderbilt [*1843 Magazine*, July 2019]

'Assessing the Impact of Closure Type on Wine Ratings and Mood' by Charles Spence and Qian Wang [*Beverages*, Vol. 3, No. 4, pp. 52, 2017]

'Giving Firms an "E" for Effort: Consumer Responses to High-Effort

Firms' by Andrea Morales [*Journal of Consumer Research*, Vol. 31, No. 4, pp. 806–812, 2005]

'The Labor Illusion: How Operational Transparency Increases Perceived Value' by Ryan Buell and Michael Norton [*Management Science*, Vol. 57, No. 9, pp. 1564–1579, 2011]

'Creating Reciprocal Value Through Operational Transparency' by Ryan Buell, Tami Kim and Chia-Jung Tsay [*Management Science*, Vol 63, No. 6, pp. 1657–2048, 2017]

4

THE GENERATION EFFECT

AS YOU CROSS the station concourse a poster catches your eye. The headline says, "OB_S_TY is a cause of cancer". It's from Cancer Research UK. You pause for a moment as you fill in the blanks.

Underneath the headline the copy gives you more detail, "Guess what is the biggest preventable cause of cancer after smoking?"

Ah, you say to yourself, obesity.

THE CANCER RESEARCH UK poster is applying a tactic from behavioural science known as the generation effect. This memory bias was first reported by Norman Slamecka and Peter Graf at the University of Toronto.

In 1978 they showed 24 students a wide range of cards featuring a set of words. Half the participants received cards with two words of similar meaning, say *rapid* and *fast*. The remainder were shown the same words, but with a twist. Only one of the pair was written in full and the other had a letter missing. So, continuing our example, the card would say *rapid* and *fas_*.

Once the subjects had read all the cards, the researchers tested their recall. The group who had generated words were 15% more likely to remember them compared with participants who had simply read the cards.

Updating the findings

The findings of the Canadian psychologists are interesting, but you might have some doubts about their validity. After all, it's a 45-year-old study based on a small student sample. And the words they studied weren't related to business or marketing.

These flaws encouraged me and Mike Treharne, at Leo Burnett, to update the study. In 2020 we asked 415 people to read the name of brands in five categories: cars, banks, beauty, supermarkets and electronics.

Some people were shown the whole word (e.g., the bank HSBC), whereas others had to generate the brand name by filling in letter blanks (e.g., the bank H_BC). Later, we asked our sample to identify which brands they had seen.

Our results supported the original findings of the 1978 study. 92% of generated words were remembered compared to 81% of ungenerated words. That makes them 14% more memorable. Or looking at it from the opposite perspective, it was two and a half times more likely that someone wouldn't remember a brand when they merely read it.

The cognitive effort involved in generating the answer makes the information stickier.

Let's look at how to apply this bias.

How can you apply this bias?

1. Apply the generation effect laterally, not just literally

The Cancer Research UK poster mentioned in the chapter introduction was a genuine ad from 2019. In this example, the generation effect is applied literally. The Graf and Slamecka experiment has been directly converted into an ad. The evidence suggests that Cancer Research UK will have boosted memorability by using the tactic. However, while they might be able to apply this tactic once or twice, it's probably too specific a tactic to be applied repeatedly.

The important thing with behavioural science experiments is not to get distracted by the superficial detail, but to focus on the key finding. The core insight for the generation effect is that involving the audience – making them exert a little effort – increases memorability.

Once you think about the insight in these broader terms, the opportunities to apply it become more widespread.

Think about David Abbott's classic ad for *The Economist*, which stated:

"I never read The Economist." Management trainee. Aged 42.

The creative hasn't removed any letters, but it still harnesses the generation effect. By making its point obliquely, the copy requires a bit of mental processing, thereby ensuring memorability. The strength of this lateral approach is that you can run a whole series of ads, whereas there are only so many times you can run ads with letters removed.

The best ads are often memorable because they make you work a little: you feel clever for figuring them out and you want to talk

THE ILLUSION OF CHOICE

about them with your friends. The skill of great creative is to balance the effort of solving the puzzle with enough stopping power to get people to pause and think.

> The best ads are often memorable because they make you work a little: you feel clever for figuring them out and you want to talk about them with your friends.

Outside of the commercial world, writers have long recognised the importance of leaving something for the audience to do. In 1956 C. S. Lewis wrote a letter to Joan Lancaster, a young fan, with the following advice on writing:

Don't use adjectives which merely tell us how you want us to feel about the thing you are describing. I mean, instead of telling us a thing was 'terrible,' describe it so that we'll be terrified. Don't say it was 'delightful'; make us say 'delightful' when we've read the description. You see, all those words (horrifying, wonderful, hideous, exquisite) are only like saying to your readers, 'Please will you do my job for me.'

2. Does asking questions harness the generation effect?

One way of balancing the competing demands of ease and effort is to pose a simple question in your copy. The mental effort involved in coming up with an answer taps into the generation effect.

However, there's another benefit: questions boost persuasiveness. The evidence comes from 2004 when Rohini Ahluwalia, from the University of Kansas and Robert Burnkrant, from Ohio State University, recruited 135 participants and showed them a series of ads.

All the ads conveyed the same information but sometimes it was communicated through a question, sometimes by a statement. So, in one example, the ad said, "Did you know that wearing Avanti shoes can reduce your risk of arthritis?" whereas the other stated, "Wearing Avanti shoes can reduce your risk of arthritis."

Finally, participants were quizzed as to their attitudes towards the ad on a series of nine-point scales. Was the ad good or bad? Favourable or unfavourable? Nice or awful?

Those who had seen the questions rated the brand 14% more positively than those who had read the statement.

Why are questions so persuasive?

Psychologists believe that questions are effective because they allow the audience to feel in control. As the author Arthur Koestler said, "The artist rules his subjects by turning them into accomplices."

Jonah Berger, a professor at the Wharton school, argues in the *Harvard Business Review* that questions tap into this idea as they shift the listener's role:

Rather than counter-arguing or thinking about all the reasons they disagree, they're sorting through their answer to your query and their feelings or opinions on the matter. And this shift increases buy-in. It encourages people to commit to the conclusion, because while people might not want to follow someone else's lead, they're more than happy to follow their own. The answer to the question isn't just any answer; it's their answer, reflecting their own personal thoughts, beliefs, and preferences. That makes it more likely to drive action.

This isn't just a theoretical argument. The tactic was harnessed by one of the greatest American political ads. When John F. Kennedy was running for the 1960 presidency, he wanted to draw attention to Richard Nixon's untrustworthy reputation.

Cleverly he avoided directly stating his opponent was dishonest as that might have stimulated reactance among voters who were potentially drawn to Nixon. (We'll discuss reactance more in Chapter 12. It's the idea that if people feel their autonomy is threatened, they often react by reasserting their freedom.) Instead, Kennedy's team created posters emblazoned with a grinning portrait of Nixon overlaid with the lines, "Would you buy a used car from this man?"

According to Jeremy Bullmore, this ad was:

A deliberate invitation to the audience to participate. Making effective use of both Nixon's slightly dodgy reputation and his shifty appearance, the creativity of the receivers is actively sought and utilised.

If you want to avoid reactance, alter your copy. Rather than making a direct statement, why don't you ask your audience a question?

3. Use your design to make people work a little bit

The final application extends the principle beyond copywriting. You can add a small amount of friction into your advertising through the design.

One experiment that investigates this idea comes from Princeton's Daniel Oppenheimer. In 2010, he conducted a study into the effect of different fonts on memorability.

He asked 28 participants to learn about three species of aliens, each of which had seven features.

However, the information was written in one of two different fonts. One version's font consisted of clean, easy-to-read block letters, whereas the other version's font consisted of italicised letters that were slightly difficult to read.

Easy-to-read font (fluent)	Hard-to-read font (disfluent)
The norgletti	*The pangerish*
• Two feet tall	• *Ten feet tall*
• Eats flower petals and pollen	• *Eats green, leafy vegetables*
• Has brown eyes	• *Has blue eyes*

Source: adapted from Oppenheimer paper.

Later, he quizzed the subjects on the information they had learned. The participants given the difficult-to-read font – the one with more friction – had much higher recall than those given the easy font. Only 73% successfully memorised text written in the easy-to-read font, compared to 87% who read the disfluent font.

The disfluent font provided just the right amount of mental friction: enough to require the brain to exert attention, without making reading so difficult that the brain gives up trying.

This is a simple tactic to apply. If the key goal for your messaging is memorability (rather than say noticeability or persuasion) then use a font that is slightly hard to read.

In this chapter, we've discussed how the generation effect can boost memorability. But behavioural scientists have identified many other ways to approach this. Another to consider is the use of rhyme. Let's look at that in the next chapter…

REFERENCES

'The generation effect: Delineation of a phenomenon' by Norman Slamecka and Peter Graf [*Journal of Experimental Psychology: Human Learning and Memory*, Vol. 4, No. 6, 592–604, 1978]

'Answering Questions about Questions: A Persuasion Knowledge Perspective for Understanding the Effects of Rhetorical Questions' by Rohini Ahluwalia and Robert Burnkrant [*Journal of Consumer Research*, Vol. 31, No. 1, pp. 26–42, 2004]

'How to Persuade People to Change Their Behaviour' by Jonah Berger [*Harvard Business Review*, April 20, 2020]

'Fortune Favors the Bold (and the Italicized): Effects of Disfluency on Educational Outcomes' by Daniel Oppenheimer, Connor Diemand-Yauman and Erikka Vaughan [*Cognition*, Vol. 118, No. 1, pp. 111–115, 2011]

5

THE KEATS
HEURISTIC

THE TRAIN IS uncomfortable and cramped. Eventually, it pulls into your station. As you step onto the platform you hear someone sneeze behind you. You flinch. It reminds you of the old ad – coughs and sneezes spread diseases.

Hoping that you have evaded your fellow passenger's nefarious attempt to spread their infection, you hurry on your way to work.

THE SLOGAN 'COUGHS and sneezes spread diseases' first ran in the US during the Spanish Flu pandemic of 1918–20 and in Britain in 1942. It's impressive that a piece of copy written more than 100 years ago is still influencing people today.

Part of the persuasiveness of the line comes from the fact it rhymes. That's the conclusion of a study conducted in 2000 by Matthew McGlone and Jessica Tofighbakhsh from Lafayette College.

The psychologists began their experiment by compiling a list of lesser-known proverbs that rhymed. They then created another doctored version that maintained the same meaning but without rhyming. You can see some examples below:

Rhyming version	Non-rhyming version
Woes unite foes	Woes unite enemies
What sobriety reveals, alcohol conceals	What sobriety reveals, alcohol unmasks
Life is mostly strife	Life is mostly struggle
Caution and measure will win you treasure	Caution and measure will win you riches
Variety prevents satiety	Variation prevents satiety

Next, McGlone and Tofighbakhsh showed 100 participants a list of 15 proverbs – randomly picking one example from each pair. So, half would have seen 'woes unite foes', whereas the other half saw 'woes unite enemies'.

After the subjects had read through the list, they were asked to rate the phrases according to how "accurate a description of human behaviour" they provided. This approach allowed the psychologists to compare the believability of the statements in the different versions.

The results were clear. The average believability of the proverbs in the non-rhyming condition was 5.26 on a 9-point scale, but 6.17 in the rhyming form. That's an improvement of 17%.

It's an impressive boost considering the meaning of the proverbs was the same in both conditions.

In the words of the psychologists this effect is "a product of the enhanced processing fluency that rhyme affords". In essence, the easier the information is to process, the more believable it becomes.

People conflate ease of processing and truth.[1] The psychologists called the greater believability of rhyming phrases the 'rhyme as reason effect' or the 'Keats heuristic'.

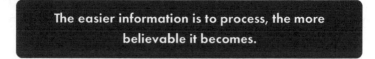

The easier information is to process, the more believable it becomes.

That's all well and good in theory, but how can you make use of the Keats heuristic?

How can you apply this bias?

1. Harness rhyme more regularly to boost believability

This finding is useful as it can help close the trust gap that separates brands and their potential customers. In 2020 IPSOS MORI asked nearly 2,000 British adults whether they trusted ad executives to generally tell the truth. Only 13% said yes. That's a worse showing than for politicians, ministers – even estate agents.

The Keats heuristic however provides a solution: use rhetorical devices like rhyme in your copy to boost believability.

This recommendation might feel like a stretch – you might worry that proverbs are too old-fashioned a technique to be

---

1   There is a long precedent for this idea. In Nietzsche's 1878 book *The Gay Science* he wrote that "the wisest among us are still occasionally fooled by rhythm – if only so far as we sometimes consider an idea truer because it has metrical form and presents itself with a divine spark and jump".

useful today. However, McGlone and Tofighbakhsh dispute that assumption.

In their paper they point to the 1994 trial of O. J. Simpson as an example of rhyme effectively persuading people in a modern setting. One of the pivotal moments in the case was when the defence lawyer, Johnnie Cochrane, argued that "if the gloves don't fit, you must acquit".

Would that argument have been as effective if he had blandly said, 'if the gloves don't fit, you must find him not guilty'? Probably not.

Of course, that's only an anecdote. But there's also experimental evidence that rhyme can improve ad effectiveness. In 2013 Petra Filkuková, from the University of Oslo, and Sven Hroar Klempe, from the Norwegian University of Science and Technology, created slogans for brands such as the clothes shop EGO and the diet course BetterLife. Sometimes their slogans rhymed, sometimes they didn't.

The psychologists showed these slogans to 183 participants, with half receiving the rhyming ones and half the alternatives. When questioned, the subjects that saw the rhyming slogans rated them as 22% more trustworthy. They were also 10% more willing to try the brands.

2. Harness rhyme to improve memorability

The benefit of rhyme stretches beyond believability; it also boosts memorability. In 2017 Alex Thompson and I ran a pilot study where we gave 36 staff at a media agency five minutes to read a list of ten statements, only half of which rhymed. Later that day we asked the subjects to return and list as many of the phrases as possible.

The results were conclusive: 29% of the rhyming statements were recalled compared to only 14% of the non-rhyming ones. That's more than a doubling of memorability.

But how valuable are these findings? Don't advertisers already know the benefits of rhyme? After all, quite a few straplines use this technique. Just have a look through the list below.

We all adore a Kia-Ora
You only get an oo with Typhoo
Easy peasy lemon squeezy
Once driven, forever smitten
For mash, get smash
It's a lot less bovver than a hover
Don't be vague, ask for Haig
Once you pop, you can't stop
No battery is stronger longer
A Mars a day helps you work, rest and play
Beanz Meanz Heinz

It's certainly a long list. But look at those lines again. What do you notice?

Did you spot that they are all more than 30 years old? The Haig line stretches back to the 1930s, the Heinz line was penned in the 60s and the Smash rhyme is from the 70s. It's far harder to think of equally iconic rhymes from the last 20 years. They have fallen out of fashion.

That's not speculation. Alex Boyd and I spent a morning in the News UK archives painstakingly categorising ads in copies of *The Times* and *The Sun* stretching back to 1977. We saw a clear pattern.

In the last decade, the number of ads with a prominent rhyme has halved. In 2007 about 4% of print ads included a rhyme compared to 10% in the 30 years prior.

Why is rhyme in decline?

But why are advertisers ignoring such a powerful technique? Perhaps because rhyme doesn't fit with marketers' motivations.

Makers of ads want their peers' admiration. That's only natural. But what gains a professional a degree of kudos is not the same as what makes for an effective ad. Our peers, other experts in advertising, are often impressed by sophisticated techniques. This leads to simple solutions, like rhyme, being derided as inferior.

Nassim Nicholas Taleb would argue this is because ad agencies don't have "skin in the game". That is, the success of an agency isn't solely a reflection of the income generated by their ads. This creates problems. In Taleb's words:

> Things designed by people without skin in the game tend to grow in complication (before their final collapse). There is absolutely no benefit for someone in such a position to propose something simple: when you are rewarded for perception, not results, you need to show sophistication. Anyone who has submitted a scholarly paper to a journal knows that you usually raise the odds of acceptance by making it more complicated than necessary.

But one theme from behavioural science is that simple solutions are often highly effective. Hopefully, a wider knowledge of behavioural science will encourage a return to tried and trusted (and simple) tactics.

So, let's finish this chapter with a few other simple tactics that affect the fluency of processing.

3. Alliteration advances accuracy

Many of the rhetorical flourishes writers and poets have used to engage their audiences through the years can boost fluency. Alliteration is one such technique.

In 2022 Hamish Bromley, Joanna Stanley and I ran a study to see if alliteration could be as effective as rhyme in boosting believability and memorability. Just like McGlone and Tofighbakhsh, we found ten relatively unknown alliterating proverbs and then rewrote them in a plainer way. You can see the full list below.

Alliterating proverb	Non-alliterating proverb
Be a worthy worker and work will come	Be a valuable worker and jobs will come
Sleep softens sorrows	Sleep lessens worries
Favour the fact, forgive the flaw	Consider the facts, overlook the mistake
He who rests grows rusty	He who rests loses ability
Great losses are great lessons	Great losses are valuable teachings
Good deeds die when discussed	Good deeds go to waste when spoken
Courage kills complications	Courage erases difficulty
Barking dogs seldom bite	Barking dogs seldom wound
A break will help you blossom	A break will help you flourish
Many men have many minds	Many men have numerous minds

The participants were shown ten proverbs – five from each list – and asked to rate how believable each one was on a nine-point scale.

When we split the data, we saw that phrases that alliterated were rated at 6.11 in terms of believability, compared to 5.72 for those that didn't. That's a 7% improvement in believability.

After the participants had completed the task, they waited a few hours, then returned and tried to remember as many proverbs as they could. This time there was a bigger difference in performance between the two types of phrase. People remembered on average 66% of the alliterating proverbs and 54% of the others. That's a 22% improvement in memorability.

4. Enhance the fluency of your brand name if you want to reduce risk perceptions

Remember that McGlone and Tofighbakhsh argued that the easier information is to process, the more believable it becomes. People conflate ease of processing and truth. However, enhancing fluency doesn't just boost believability. According to Hyunjin Song and Norbert Schwarz from the University of Michigan, it can also affect people's evaluation of risk.

In 2009 they showed participants a list of fictitious food additives. Some of the names were hard to pronounce, such as Hnegripitrom, whereas others were easy to pronounce, such as Magnalroxate. The psychologists then asked the subjects to indicate how harmful they thought the additives were on a seven-point scale – with one indicating the drug was very safe and seven that it was very harmful.

Additives with hard to pronounce names received an average score of 4.12, compared to 3.70 for easier to pronounce words. That's an 11% increase in perceived harmfulness for hard to pronounce words.

The psychologists argued that ease of pronunciation was conflated with risk. This insight can easily be applied by advertisers

– if you want to reassure your customers that your drug or new launch is low risk, make sure you choose an easy to pronounce brand name.

However, there may be occasions when you want to emphasise how exciting or risky your product is. In that case you want to give your product a hard to pronounce name. In fact, the psychologists tested this idea with fictitious theme park rides. They found those rides with hard to pronounce names were judged riskier – but also more exciting.

5. Tailor the font you use to your task

Song and Schwarz's research extends beyond word choice to more visual effects. In 2008, they studied the influence of font choice on processing fluency and perceptions of ease. In their experiment, they gave 20 participants the following exercise instructions:

> Tuck your chin into your chest and then lift your chin upwards as far as possible. 6–10 repetitions.

Some participants were given the instructions in an easy-to-read font (Arial, 12 point), others had to read the information in a difficult to read font (Brush, 12 point).

Arial   *Brush*

The group that received the fluent, easy-to-read font thought the exercise would take 8.2 minutes, whereas the other group estimated 15.1 minutes. That's almost a doubling of perceived effort.

In the words of the psychologists:

People misread the difficulty of reading the exercise instructions as indicative of the difficulty involved in doing the exercise... people are sensitive to their feelings of ease or difficulty, but insensitive to where these feelings come from. As a result, they misattribute the experienced ease or difficulty to whatever is in the focus of their attention.

Once again, these findings have a practical implication. If you want people to perceive a task as easy, write in an easy-to-read font, whereas if you want to emphasise the difficulty, a harder-to-read font is more appropriate.

Consider the case of dining – if you're a meal kit provider, an easy-to-read font like Arial would help you persuade consumers that your dish will be simple and easy to prepare. However, if you're running a high-end restaurant, you may have different motivations. You probably want to emphasise how much effort has gone into the preparation of your sophisticated dishes. If so, you should use a more difficult to read font.

Although psychologists have only recently proven in controlled conditions the power of rhyme and alliteration, it's something that poets have known intuitively for millennia.

In fact, there's much that academics and advertisers can learn from ancient writers. Next, we're going to turn to a tactic used as far back as Homer and Cicero: the power of concrete language. Read on to find out more...

REFERENCES

'Birds of a feather flock conjointly (?): Rhyme as reason in aphorisms' by Matthew McGlone and Jessica Tofighbakhsh [*Psychological Science*, Vol. 11, No. 5, pp. 424–428, 2000]

'Rhyme as reason in commercial and social advertising' by Petra Filkuková and Sven Hroar Klempe [*Scandinavian Journal of Psychology*, Vol. 54, No. 5, pp. 423–431, 2013]

Skin In The Game: Hidden Asymmetries in Daily Life by Nicholas Taleb [2018]

'If it's difficult to pronounce, it must be risky: Fluency, familiarity and risk perception' by Hyunjin Song and Norbert Schwarz [*Psychological Science*, Vol. 20, No. 1, pp. 135–138, 2009]

'If it's hard to read, it's hard to do: Processing Fluency affects effect prediction and motivation' by Hyunjin Song and Norbert Schwarz [*Psychological Science*, Vol. 19, No. 10, pp. 986–988, 2008]

6

CONCRETENESS

SOON AFTER YOU arrive at work, you have a meeting in the boardroom with potential clients.

When you enter, the room is full. Your boss, Jane, is struggling valiantly to load up the slides. So, to fill the time, you introduce yourself to everyone there, vigorously shaking hands and making small talk.

When you introduce yourself to the final client, she reminds you that you've met before.

Twice.

You splutter an apology.

YOU SHOULDN'T FEEL embarrassed about forgetting a face. You're not alone; the vast majority of information we take in is quickly forgotten.

In fact, the fallibility of memory is perhaps the oldest finding in psychology, with studies stretching as far back as 1885 and the work of the German psychologist Hermann Ebbinghaus. He coined the term 'the forgetting curve' to describe the rate at which we forget information. It tends to follow a predictable pattern: the biggest drop in retention happens soon after we learn new facts. Over time, more is forgotten, but at a slower rate.

Even though the forgetting curve was discovered more than 100 years ago it still occurs today. Jaap Murre, from the University of Amsterdam, reran Ebbinghaus's experiments in 2015 and found similar results.

But Ebbinghaus didn't just describe our forgetfulness, he also came up with tactics to overcome it. Most notably, he discovered that the rate of forgetting can be slowed by re-reading the material at regular intervals. But repetition, while effective, is an expensive tactic for marketers. Luckily, there are other, less costly, findings from behavioural science that can aid memory.

> Repetition, while effective, is an expensive tactic for marketers. Luckily, there are other, less costly, findings from behavioural science that can aid memory.

However, before we discuss the research let's do a little exercise. I've put together a list of two-word phrases. Please read through them slowly, and then cover them up:

square door
impossible amount
rusty engine
better excuse
flaming forest
apparent fact
muscular gentleman

common fate
white horse
subtle fault

Now, try writing down as many as possible. There's no rush, I'll wait...

Which words did you recall? My bet is that you found it easiest to bring to mind concrete phrases, those describing things that exist physically, like 'square door' and 'muscular gentleman'. In contrast, the abstract ones, like 'common fate' or 'better excuse', most likely slipped your mind.

If that's true, your experience is typical according to Ian Begg, a psychologist at the University of Western Ontario. In 1972 he recruited 25 students and read them a list of 20 two-word phrases, including the ones you've just read. He then asked the subjects to recall as many as they could.

The results were stark. People remembered 9% of the abstract words and 36% of the concrete words. A striking four-fold difference.

The scale of Begg's findings is impressive, but you might have concerns about its validity from a commercial perspective. First, the sample: 25 students is a worryingly small number of potentially unrepresentative people.

Second, the word choice: phrases like 'rusty engine' and 'muscular gentleman' don't often appear in advertising (not before the watershed anyway).

Finally, the timings: in Begg's experiment he asked people to recall the terms immediately after he read them out. That's interesting, but brands normally need messages to be remembered for substantially longer.

Because of these flaws, in 2021 Mike Treharne, from Leo Burnett, and I reran Begg's study with a few tweaks. We began by recruiting a more robust 425-strong sample. We then gave our subjects a list of ten phrases, some abstract and some concrete. All of the phrases could feasibly appear in commercial communications.

Some of the phrases were concrete, such as:

fast car
skinny jeans
cashew nut
money in your pocket
happy hens

Others were abstract, such as:

innovative quality
trusted provenance
central purpose
wholesome nutrition
ethical vision

Finally, we tweaked the timings. Instead of asking people to recall the phrases immediately after hearing them, we introduced a five-minute delay. That's not as long as ads need to be remembered, but it's a step closer to reality.

The results were even more pronounced than in the original study. Participants remembered 6.7% of the concrete phrases, but just 0.7% of the abstract ones. That's a ten-fold difference. The findings about concreteness aren't just a quirk of Begg's study.

These lab studies are also supported by real-world evidence. The book, *Made to Stick*, describes analysis of ancient stories conducted by Michael Havelock, a classicist at Yale. Havelock has shown that stories that have been passed down by word of mouth, such as the *Odyssey* and the *Iliad* have plenty of concrete words but few abstractions. His argument is that when the tales were recounted, the concrete parts were remembered while the abstractions were forgotten and disappeared.

Is sight the 'keenest of senses'?

But what explains the difference in memorability between these styles of communicating? Begg suggests that concrete phrases are stickier because they can be visualised.

This idea has long roots. Returning to the classical world, the Roman orator Cicero said in 55 BC:

The keenest of all our senses is the sense of sight, and consequently perceptions received by the ears or from other sources can most easily be remembered if they are conveyed to our minds by the mediation of vision.

So Cicero, like Begg, suggests that when we are exposed to an idea, we have better recall if we're able to picture an image in our mind's eye.

So let's look at how concreteness can work for you.

How can you apply this bias?

1. Mind your language

The study I conducted with Mike Treharne showed a huge swing in recall – nearly a ten-fold difference. Considering many studies into other biases record an effect of 10% or 20% it's important to make sure you apply this idea rather than just read about it.

Luckily, applying it is simple: whenever possible, strip your copy of abstract language and replace it with concrete terminology.

If that recommendation is unclear, let me give you an example. Think about Apple's early iPod advertising. While other mp3 players of the day trumpeted their storage size in megabytes, Apple made it real with "1,000 songs in your pocket". The consumer was able to picture the device in their jeans pocket, easily storing all their favourite tunes. That act of visualisation helped cement the claim in the mind.

Apple's preference for concrete language is rare. Far too many brands are attracted to vague abstractions, like Rightmove's "Find Your Happy" or Hitachi's "Inspire the next".

However, the popularity of forgettable abstractions in copy is an opportunity for you. A simple copy tweak can make your brand more memorable than most of the competition.

2. Help your customer imagine using your product

Using language that can be pictured makes your writing more memorable. But there are added benefits to encouraging potential customers to visualise using your product.

In 2011, Ryan Elder from Brigham Young University and Aradhna Krishna from the University of Michigan conducted a study into this idea, or what they called 'perceptual fluency'.

The researchers showed 321 participants an image of a delicious-looking slice of cake, with a fork on either the left or the right side of the plate. Participants were then asked whether they were left- or right-handed, and to indicate their purchase intent.

Source: Tom Shotton.

When handedness matched the orientation of the cutlery – that is when right-handed people saw the fork placed on the right side – participants had 35% higher purchase intentions towards the cake. The authors concluded that lining up the fork in a manner that was natural for the viewer encouraged them to imagine eating it, and the pleasure this gave boosted purchase intent.

So, wherever possible help your customer imagine using your product – whether that's through tweaks to your imagery, language or even using more hi-tech approaches like augmented reality.

However, as with all studies there are nuances. In 2011, Elder conducted a similar experiment with a series of soup ads. This time though he varied the attractiveness of the dish: some people saw an appealing flavour (Asiago cheese and tomato), whereas others saw an unpleasant one (cottage cheese and tomato).

When he made it easier to imagine tasting the soup (he used the same mechanic he used with the cake, but this time with spoons rather than forks) he saw an interesting result. If the product was desirable the purchase intent went up by 24% but, if it was undesirable, intent dropped by 26%.

It seems that perceptual fluency, like the illusion of effort, has a multiplicative effect – easily imagining trying the pleasant-sounding soup made it even more desirable. But imagining sampling the unpleasant soup made it even less desirable.

3. Keep it simple, stupid

Another benefit of using concrete language is that it tends to be simple. And simple language reflects well on the communicator.

Evidence for this idea comes from the Princeton psychologist Daniel Oppenheimer in a paper that has possibly the best ever title: 'Consequences of Erudite Vernacular Utilized Irrespective of Necessity: Problems with Using Long Words Needlessly'.[1]

In this study, participants read samples of text including graduate school applications, sociology dissertation abstracts and translations of a work of Descartes. Some participants read the original version which was written in a verbose, jargon-filled style, while others were given an edited version where the unnecessarily complex words had been switched for simpler alternatives.

Finally, the psychologist asked the participants to rate the intelligence of the authors. Those who read the simplified version scored the authors 13% higher than those who read the more complex, original text.

This finding is valuable as it runs counter to much brand behaviour.

---

[1] While most academic journal titles are bland, Oppenheimer isn't the only academic to add in a rare flash of humour. For example, there's 'Fantastic yeasts and where to find them: the hidden diversity of dimorphic fungal pathogens' by Marley Van Dyke, which appeared in the journal *Current Opinion in Microbiology* in 2019. Or a paper written by Erika Carlson in the *Journal of Personality and Social Psychology* from 2011: 'You probably think this paper's about you: Narcissists' perceptions of their personality and reputation.' There's even a 2017 paper in the *American Journal on Addictions* by Heather Oxentine, 'Medical Marijuana: Can't We All Just Get a Bong?'

According to the language consultancy *Linguabrand*, the average reading age of the UK population is 13.5, but the average reading age of brand websites is 17.5. This, they argue, isn't just a factor of the subject matter – after all the *Financial Times* communicates far more complex matters but at an average reading age of 16. Instead, it's explained by a lingering misapprehension: too many professionals believe complexity signals intelligence. Unfortunately, the evidence points in the opposite direction.

So even if you can't use concrete words then at least keep the abstractions as simple as possible. You'll be in good company. The German philosopher Arthur Schopenhauer was an advocate of simplicity. He famously said, "One should use common words to say uncommon things."[2]

4. Stories over statistics

There's evidence that you can also apply the principle of concreteness by prioritising stories over statistics. In 2007 Deborah Small, George Loewenstein and Paul Slovic investigated how communications could be adapted to boost charitable giving. In particular, they were interested in whether tales about individual suffering were more motivating than messages describing a tragedy in statistical terms.

The psychologists paid 121 people $5 to take part in the experiment. As part of the study the participants read a description of food shortages in Africa.

Some read a passage which described the victims in statistical terms (e.g., "Food shortages in Malawi are affecting more than three million children..."). Others were given a story that focused on an

---

2 Churchill (who won the Nobel Prize for literature as well as being a great war leader) made a similar remark. He argued that "Short words are best, and old words when short are best of all."

individual (e.g., "Any money that you donate will go to Rokia, a seven-year-old girl from Mali, Africa. Rokia is desperately poor and faces a threat of severe hunger or even starvation…").

At the end of the experiment the participants had the option to donate some of their fee to a charity, Save the Children.

Those who had read about the individual's story donated $2.83 on average, more than double the $1.17 given by those who had heard the statistics. The psychologists termed this the 'identifiable victim effect'.

These findings relate to the Begg study. Statistics often leave an audience unmoved because they are hard to relate to. It's impossible to imagine three million people. Whereas when we think of Rokia an image springs to mind immediately. We can relate to the human-sized scale of a single victim, and that engenders more emotion and bigger donations.

This insight was recognised by Stalin, who supposedly remarked with his typical savagery, "If only one man dies of hunger, that is a tragedy. If millions die, that's only statistics."[3]

So, where possible shun statistics and make your tale relatable on a human level.

5. Check your expertise

All these studies raise a question: why don't more brands use concrete language?

Perhaps because marketers are experts in their category. Whether it's cars or chocolate bars, a marketer and its agency team will be immersed in the details of the business. That's a problem as, according to Chip and Dan Heath in their book *Made to Stick*:

---

3 Interestingly, Mother Teresa, who seems as far removed from Stalin as it's possible to get, said something similar: "If I look at the mass, I will never act. If I look at the one, I will."

The difference between an expert and a novice is the ability to think abstractly. New jurors are struck by the lawyer's personalities and factual details and courtroom rituals. Meanwhile, judges weigh the current case against the abstract lessons of past cases and legal precedent.

So, remember that your expertise might make it hard to spot that you're slipping into abstractions. What appears easily understandable, even visualisable, to you, might not be to your customer – who is less of a category expert.

A final side effect of communicating in a concrete, rather than abstract, manner is that it steers you away from generalities towards more precise details. That precision has its own set of benefits. Let's turn to them now...

REFERENCES

'Replication and Analysis of Ebbinghaus' Forgetting Curve' by Jaap Murre and Jorei Dros [*PLoS ONE*, Vol. 10, No. 7, 2015]

'Recall of meaningful phrases' by Ian Begg [*Journal of Verbal Learning and Verbal Behaviour*, Vol. 11, No. 4, pp. 431–439, 1972]

Made to Stick: Why Some Ideas Survive and Others Die by Chip Heath and Dan Heath [2007]

'The "Visual Depiction Effect" in Advertising: Facilitating Embodied Mental Simulation through Product Orientation' by Ryan Elder and Aradhna Krishna [*Journal of Consumer Research*, Vol, 38, No. 6, pp. 998–1003, 2012]

'Consequences of Erudite Vernacular Utilized Irrespective of Necessity: Problems with Using Long Words Needlessly' by Daniel Oppenheimer [*Applied Cognitive Psychology*, Vol. 20, No. 2, pp. 139–156, 2006]

'Sympathy and callousness: The impact of deliberative thought on donations to identifiable and statistical victims' by Deborah Small, George Loewenstein and Paul Slovic [*Organizational Behavior and Human Decision Processes*, Vol, 102, No. 2, pp. 143–153, 2007]

6 ½

PRECISION

YOU'RE FEELING IN need of a break after a slightly awkward client meeting. So you decide to treat yourself. There's an interesting-looking independent bookstore near the office that you've been meaning to check out.

As you wander in, your eyes skim the titles of the books on display. One jumps out at you: *The History of the World in 10½ Chapters*.

Your curiosity is piqued. Why 10½? Not 10 chapters, not 11, but 10½...

THE NUMBER CAUGHT your eye because it's distinctive. Since most books use round numbers, a precise number is more noticeable. Evidence for this assertion comes from Michael Santos, a psychologist at the University of California. In 1994 he ran a study in which scruffily dressed researchers pretended to be beggars. Sometimes they asked passers-by for money in a standard manner – either requesting a quarter or more vaguely any loose change. Sometimes they asked for a novel amount, either 17c or 35c. Santos found that people were 60% more likely to give money when the researchers asked for the novel amount. He argued that a precise request disrupted people's expectations and boosted noticeability. He called this finding the pique effect.

Precision has similar benefits for brands.

Think about Heinz. In 1896 the founder, Henry J. Heinz, decided to emblazon his packaging with the claim that his company had 57 varieties. Even then, the company had far more lines, but he was untroubled by this fact – it was the precision that he loved.

Or consider an even older claim from Ivory soaps. From 1895 they stated they were 99 44/100% pure.

Would these claims have grabbed the public consciousness if they had been blander – 60 varieties of beans or 100% pure soap?

Specific rather than round numbers

But these precise numbers have a value beyond their distinctiveness. Statistics are judged to be more believable if they're specific.

The evidence for this comes from a 2006 study by Robert Schindler from Rutgers University and Richard Yalch from the University of Washington. The psychologists showed 199 participants an ad for a fictitious body spray and then asked them about the accuracy and credibility of the claims.

The twist was that sometimes the ad stated that the deodorant "Lasts 50% longer than any other deodorant". On other occasions they changed the statistic to a more precise number: either 47% or 53%.

This subtle tweak boosted perceived accuracy and credibility. Precise claims were judged to be roughly 10% more accurate than round claims. Credibility ratings were slightly higher for precise claims than for rounded ones, but this effect was not statistically significant.

So what explains the power of precision? The most likely explanation is one of association. Over time people notice that those who are sure of themselves give precise details, whereas those who are uncertain take refuge in vague estimations.

For example, imagine if someone asked you the age of your partner? You would be able to answer exactly – you'd say 35 or 46, or whatever was the case. But what if the questioner asked your cousin's age? Well, then you would probably answer more vaguely. You might say they were in their thirties or forties.

This association between specificity and accuracy becomes so strong that people use it as a quick rule of thumb when evaluating a statement. In fact it's so strong a link that, as Schindler shows, precision is used as a guide even when it's unrelated to accuracy.

Consider, for example, how you might perceive a friend if, rather than saying, "I'll be back in a half-hour," the friend said, "I'll be back in 27 minutes." Santos, Leve, and Pratkanis (1994) found that a panhandler can get more money by asking for 17 or 37 cents rather than requesting a quarter. Although they explained this phenomenon by the attention-getting properties of the sharp numbers, the results of the present study would suggest an alternative explanation. It may be that when one is approached for 37 cents, the sharpness of the number suggests that there is a very specific need, say, that the requestor is only a few cents short of what he needs to buy a bus ticket home. By contrast, the request for a round amount of money might suggest that there is no specific need – rather, the requestor just wants money.

> The association between specificity and accuracy is so strong that people use it as a quick rule of thumb when evaluating a statement.

Now that we've explored the value of precision, let's see how you can use it to improve your ads.

How can you apply this bias?

1. Apply the power of precision

These findings about precision are interesting as they run counter to how most brands behave. For convenience, they tend to round their statistics. A popular insurance brand might claim for example that it has 'Over one million customers'. Or an advertising book might claim that it covers 25 behavioural biases that influence what you buy.

However, Schindler's work suggests they're both making a mistake. The insurance brand should embrace precision, for example by saying, 'Over 1.15m customers'. Or perhaps the author could release a follow-up, offering another 16½ behavioural biases.

Again, this research provides you with an opportunity. Communicate more precisely and harness the boost to believability.

2. Convey value through precise pricing

The benefit of precise numbers stretches beyond believability. When it comes to prices, they also convey better value.

Two University of Florida psychologists, Chris Janiszewski and

Dan Uy, published a simple experiment into pricing in the academic journal *Psychological Science* in 2008.

The psychologists told participants the asking price for a series of goods, including cheese, a beach house, a figurine, a pet rock and a plasma TV. The participants then had to estimate the wholesale cost of the items. The twist in the experiment was that while some participants were given a round asking price, others had a precise one.

For example, a third of the participants were told that the cheese cost $5, the next third that it cost $4.85 and the final third that it cost $5.15. Their estimate of the actual value was respectively $3.75, $4.17 and $4.41.

This pattern occurred for each of the items tested. The participants invariably thought that rounded prices were marked-up to a higher degree than precise numbers.

The psychologists hypothesised that buyers know that prices are marked up. The difference between round and precise pricing is found in the degree to which buyers think the price has been inflated. When they're thinking about a round price, say £10 for a watch, they tend to adjust down in large increments – for example, from £10 to £9. In contrast, when they are considering precise figures, their units shrink so they adjust down in smaller amounts, so for a £10.25 toaster they might perceive its worth at £10.15 or £10.05.

The psychologists corroborated their findings in the real world by analysing 25,564 house sales from Alachua County, Florida. They discovered that sellers who set a precise asking price – say $799,499 rather than $800,000 – sold their home for closer to the asking price than those who opted for a rounded figure.

The impact of precision on the perception of price will be of interest to many marketers. After all, what brand doesn't want to appear better value? However, there are plenty of other pricing tactics psychologists that have identified.

The next chapter is a bonus one and in it we'll discuss the power of giving people additional content rather than a discounted price...

REFERENCES

'It Seems Factual, But Is It? Effects of Using Sharp versus Round Numbers in Advertising Claims' by Robert Schindler and Richard Yalch [*Advances in Consumer Research*, Vol. 33, pp. 586–590, 2006]

'Precision of the Anchor Influences the Amount of Adjustment' by Chris Janiszewski and Dan Uy [*Psychological Science*, Vol. 19, No. 2, pp. 121–127, 2008]

BONUS CHAPTER: BASE VALUE NEGLECT

YOU FIND YOURSELF scanning through the business section. A yellow and black book stands out from the otherwise drab fare on the table.

The blurb looks vaguely interesting and there are a couple of positive reviews on the back. Best of all, a message on the front cover announces that this new edition comes with a bonus chapter – that's 4% extra free.

Happy with your bargain, you take it over to the till to pay.

YOUR ATTENTION WAS caught by the bonus content. This tactic of including additional extras for free is sometimes used by brands, but it's less common than simply offering a small discount.

> The tactic of including additional extras for free is sometimes used by brands, but it's less common than simply offering a small discount.

Are brands missing a trick in favouring discounts? Well, this bonus chapter investigates that very point.

The most authoritative study on this topic comes from Akshay Rao from the University of Minnesota and Haipeng Chen from Texas A&M University. In 2012 they investigated the impact of different types of promotional activity on the sales of hand lotion at a local shop. During the first week, the shop sold the lotion at a 35% discount on the regular price, on the second week they sold the same item for the same price but described it as a bonus pack with 50% free. The messaging alternated for 16 weeks.

Economically, these two offers are similar. The price discount is actually the slightly better deal so we would expect that to be more popular. However, that's not what happened.

In fact, when the bonus message ran, 27 hand lotions were sold, whereas when the discount message ran, that number dropped to 15. That's a difference of 81%. Even though the test involved a small sales volume, the scale of the variation meant it was a statistically significant finding.

But why was the bonus message more effective? In the words of the authors:

Consumers' preference for a bonus pack over an economically equivalent price discount is systematically affected by a tendency to neglect the base value associated with percentages.

By that, they mean that shoppers tend to focus too much on the headline percentage, that is the 35% or the 50%, and forget about the equally important matter of the base that the percentage refers to. In this case, since 50 is a bigger number than 35, people assumed it was preferable.

How can you apply this bias?

1. Test emphasising bonuses rather than discounts

It's more common for brands to try and influence shoppers by offering discounts on their products rather than added extras. However, the experiment by Rao and Chen suggests that they might be making a mistake. In their study framing the offer as a larger bonus pack was the most effective intervention.

The study was only small scale, so you might want to run your own experiment to test this idea.

2. Harness base neglect beyond pricing

Rao argues that the principle of base value neglect can be extended to services. He gives the example of United Airlines, whose flights from San Francisco to Sydney take 15 hours. If they wanted to highlight improvements, United Airlines would do better to emphasise those relating to an increase in speed, say 25%, rather than the equivalent decrease in time taken, say 20%.

Alternatively, a car manufacturer could describe improvements in energy efficiency, say a 50% increase in miles per gallon, rather than emphasise the decline in energy consumption, say the equivalent 33% decrease in fuel consumption.

However, all this discussion of base rate neglect is a digression. Let's get back to the main book and another quirk of pricing known as extremeness aversion...

REFERENCES

'When More is Less: The Impact of Base Value Neglect on Consumer Preferences for Bonus Packs Over Price Discounts' by Haipeng (Allan) Chen, Howard Marmorstein, Michael Tsiros & Akshay Rao [*Journal of Marketing, Vol. 76.* No. 4, pp. 64–77, 2012]

7

EXTREMENESS
AVERSION

AFTER RETURNING FROM the bookshop, you settle down to your main task this morning: a presentation for your boss, Sophia. As you're googling for images for the deck, your attention is piqued by a banner ad for an international children's charity. They're raising funds to help victims of war, so you decide to contribute.

After clicking on the appeal you're taken through to the online donation page. It has defaulted to the monthly regular giving option. There are three amounts to choose from: £27, £18 or £7.

You hesitate for a few moments and then pick the middle option.

YOU SHOULDN'T BE too surprised by your decision. There's a well-known finding in behavioural science that when faced with three price options people tend to pick the middle

THE ILLUSION OF CHOICE

one.[1] In situations of uncertainty people assume the lowest-priced option is likely to be poor quality and that picking it might make them look a bit mean, whereas the highest priced option is likely to be overpriced and they might look like a show-off. This idea is known as extremeness aversion.

It's worth experimenting with this bias at your company, as extremeness aversion is a robust finding. Ulf Böckenholt from Northwestern University conducted a meta-analysis in 2015 and found evidence for the impact of extremeness aversion across 142 studies.

B2B as well as B2C

Most of the academic research is conducted among consumers. However, this bias can be harnessed when targeting professionals too. In 2018, along with the agency The Marketing Practice, I questioned 213 decision-makers at companies to see how affected they were by behavioural biases.

One area that we looked at was extremeness aversion. We asked the respondents:

Imagine that your company is looking to hire a cleaning service. There are different options available depending on how often you want them to come. Which option do you pick?

Half the respondents were shown these three options:

1. Cleaner comes once a week (four hours per day) – £1,872 (+VAT) per year.

---

1   I briefly discussed extremeness aversion in *The Choice Factory*. However, I didn't have a chance to cover the nuances of the bias in that book. Since it's a bias with such practical implications I wanted to rectify that.

2. Cleaner comes three days a week (four hours per day) – £5,616 (+VAT) per year.

3. Cleaner comes every weekday (four hours per day) – £9,360 (+VAT) per year.

In this scenario 18% of people chose the pricey 'every weekday' option.

The next half of the respondents were given a slightly different mix of options:

1. Cleaner comes three days a week (four hours per day) – £5,616 (+VAT) per year.

2. Cleaner comes every weekday (four hours per day) – £9,360 (+VAT) per year.

3. Cleaner comes for the full day every weekday (seven hours per day) – £16,384 (+VAT) per year.

In this scenario, the number of people choosing the 'every weekday' option more than doubled to 37%. Even though the inherent attributes of the offer hadn't changed, its appeal varied according to its relative position.

Next, we'll look at several ways to leverage extremeness aversion to your benefit.

How can you apply this bias?

1. Launch a super-premium option

It's easy to apply this finding. Say you're selling two variants of your brand – a basic one and a higher-margin premium one. You can encourage sales of the premium line by introducing a super-premium version.

If you do, you'll be in good company. Have a look at the following image from Tide's website. Tide's premium Cashback package has a value beyond its direct sales. It encourages people to upgrade from the Free to Plus accounts.

Tide applying extremeness aversion to their business accounts.

2. Make sure you harness extremeness aversion if you have a utilitarian product or an older target audience

The meta-analysis by Böckenholt identified that although extremeness aversion was a broadly applicable finding there were significant variations in the scale of its impact.

One key variation is by product type. In his study, he differentiated between the effect of extremeness aversion on utilitarian products, such as microwaves and detergent, and hedonic ones, such as chocolate and designer watches. People were much more likely to opt for the middle option with utilitarian purchases where pain avoidance was a key driver, rather than hedonic purchases, where pleasure seeking was more important.

The second relevant finding is that extremeness aversion tends to increase with age. In unpublished research from 2015, UCLA Anderson's Aimee Drolet and the University of Chicago's Reid Hastie asked 282 adults to make a series of choices.[2] They presented the audience with choices in a diverse range of categories, stretching from baseball tickets to ice cream and binoculars. The psychologists found that older adults were most likely to pick the middle option, doing so 61% of the time compared to 41% for youngsters.

So, if you are working with a utilitarian product, or one that targets older consumers, make sure that extremeness aversion is part of your arsenal.

3. Consider the order in which you display products

Extremeness aversion is applied reasonably regularly by brands. However, the way that brands apply it could be improved. For example, it can be combined with a bias called the 'order effect' for maximum potency.

---

2 The unpublished study can be found in this 2017 paper by Itamar Simonson from Stanford and his colleagues (page 6): https://tinyurl.com/h279yyxz.

> Extremeness aversion can be combined with a bias called the 'order effect' for maximum potency.

The best way to explain this finding is to turn to an experiment. In 2012, Donald Lichtenstein from Colorado University and his team ran an eight-week experiment in a bar in the States.

When drinkers arrived at the bar, they were given a menu of 13 bottled beers. Sometimes the staff handed out a menu with a $4 beer at the top and progressively more expensive beers below. On other occasions the same drinks were listed but in descending price order.

The psychologists found that when the menu had a low-priced item at the top the average price paid was $5.78. But when the menu order was flipped the average price paid rose by 24c to $6.02 – a statistically significant 4% increase.

But why? Well, the psychologists argued that people tend to read the menu from top to bottom, and the first price you spot has a disproportionate impact in determining what's a reasonable amount to pay. If you spy an expensive beer first, the mid-priced one that you see later feels like a bargain. Whereas if you spot a cheap beer first it reframes the middle-priced one as an extravagance.

The psychologists ran further studies in other categories to test the validity of the results. For example, they gave 219 participants a list of pens they could buy, with prices ranging from 15c to 90c. The average purchase price was 63c when the prices were shown in descending order, compared to 53c paid in the ascending condition. That's a 19% increase.

Again, these findings have practical implications. Let's return to Tide and their three products. According to the order effect, the ideal approach would be to flip the sequence. Since people read from left to right, they should position the most expensive one on the far left.[3]

4. Consider the decoy effect:
a twist on extremeness aversion

Extremeness aversion isn't the only way to harness price relativity. An alternative strategy is the 'decoy effect'.[4]

The first study into this bias was run in 1982 by psychologists Joel Huber, John Payne and Christopher Puto from Duke University. Huber and his colleagues asked 153 participants to make choices between a selection of beers.

Some participants were shown two beers:

Beer A, priced at $1.80 and rated at 50 out of 100 in terms of quality.

Beer B, priced at $2.60 and rated 70 out of 100.

In this scenario, neither of the options is obviously better: Beer A is cheaper, but Beer B is better quality. There's no objectively superior option. This led to a pretty even split in choices: 43% of participants chose Beer A and 57% Beer B.

Next, a second group of participants were shown three beers:

---

3 This isn't the only experiment into the importance of the order. Reid Hastie from the University of Chicago has shown that, all things being equal, people tend to prefer the first item on a list. In 2009 he asked 214 participants to taste between two and five wines. Although they were told they would be trying different wines, all of the samples were the same. At the end of the tasting, each participant was asked which wine was their favourite. The first wine was always the preferred choice. Another reason to make sure that your audience sees the item you want them to purchase first.

4 This effect is sometimes known as asymmetric dominance.

Beer A, priced at $1.80 and rated at 50 out of 100 in terms of quality.

Beer B, priced at $2.60 and rated 70 out of 100.

Beer C, priced at $1.80 and rated at 40 out of 100.

In this scenario Beer C is the decoy. It's similar to Beer A but obviously less attractive: it's the same price but worse quality. In the words of the psychologists, Beer A 'dominates' C. In this scenario 63% of participants chose Beer A – an increase of 47%. As we have seen elsewhere people often prefer a quick and simple decision – even if it's suboptimal – over a complex but accurate one. The participants' attention is drawn to the simple comparison between A and C at the expense of the less easily comparable option of B.

This bias is easy to apply. Let's consider the Tide example again. One way to steer people towards the £49.99 option would be to include an option that was priced the same but had markedly fewer benefits.

Big brands aren't the only ones to apply this tactic. According to Rory Sutherland, estate agents:

... exploit this effect by showing you a decoy house, to make it easier for you to choose one of the two houses they really want to sell you. They typically show you a totally inappropriate house and then two comparable houses, of which one is clearly better value than the other. The better value house is the one they want to sell you, while the other is shown to you for the purpose of making the final house seem really good.

As with extremeness aversion there are variations in the impact of this bias. One factor that seems to impact the scale of the effect is the age of the target. Sunghan Kim and Lynn Hasher from the University of Toronto ran a study in 2005 with 689 students (aged between 17 and 27 years old) and 384 older adults (aged between 60 and 79). The researchers found that the bias was most effective with the younger group. They argued that increased age, and the category experience that arises from that, reduced the impact of the bias.

The decoy effect and extremeness aversion are well-known biases. But that's not the case with all pricing studies. Have you ever heard of denominator neglect? If not, you might be interested in the next chapter...

REFERENCES

'A meta-analysis of extremeness aversion' by Nico Neumann, Ulf Böckenholt and Ashish Sinha [*Journal of Consumer Psychology*, Vol. 26, No. 2, pp. 193–212, 2015]

Behavioural Science: What does it mean for B2B marketers by The Marketing Practice and Richard Shotton [2018] retrieved from: https://25865525. fs1.hubspotusercontent-eu1.net/hubfs/25865525/Blogs/Reports/ Behavioural-Science-for-B2B-marketers-TMP-research.pdf

'The influence of Price Presentation Order on Consumer Choice' by Kwanho Suk, Jiheon Lee and Donald Lichenstein [*Journal of Marketing Research*, Vol. 49, No. 5, pp. 708–717, 2012]

'Adding Asymmetrically Dominated Alternatives: Violations of Regularity and the Similarity Hypothesis' by Joel Huber, John W Payne and Christopher Puto [*Journal of Consumer Research*, Vol. 9, No. 1, pp. 90–98, 1982]

'The Attraction Effect in Decision Making: Superior Performance by Older Adults' by Sunghan Kim and Lynn Hasher [*Quarterly Journal of Experimental Psychology*, Vol. 58, No. 1, pp. 120–133, 2005]

8

DENOMINATOR
NEGLECT

TODAY IS FEELING like a bit of a struggle, so you pop to the office kitchen to make yourself a strong cup of coffee. You bump into your colleague Anna, who is selling tickets for a sweepstake for your company charity.

There are two options – there's a sweepstake just for your team or one that the whole company is taking part in. The prize is the same – a day off work – and the ticket price is the same too. For the team sweepstake there'll be one prize for your ten-person unit, whereas for the company one there'll be nine prizes for the 100 staff.

You think about buying both tickets, but at £5 a pop they're pretty pricey and payday was a while ago. Best to pick just one.

But which one? You deliberate for a couple of seconds and then plump for the company-wide sweepstake – with nine chances to win, it could be you. You hand over a crumpled fiver and then head back to your desk, daydreaming about what you'll do on your bonus day off.

D ID YOU MAKE the right choice? A dispassionate evaluation of the odds suggests not. Have a look at the underlying odds of the two different sweepstakes: the sweepstake just for your team offered a 10% chance of winning, compared to 9% for the office-wide option.

You'd not be alone in making that error. Daniel Kahneman was first to label this phenomenon "denominator neglect", in his book *Thinking, Fast and Slow*. This is the tendency to fixate on the headline number, in our case the one or nine winners, rather than what that number represents, a 10% or 9% chance of winning. There have since been a number of studies into denominator neglect. In the words of psychologist David Bourdin:

It appears that individuals are biased towards choices with large absolute frequencies of success, rather than large probabilities of success.

If that sounds a little woolly, then let me take you through a study to clear things up.

> We tend to fixate on the headline number, rather than what that number represents.

In 1994, Veronika Denes-Raj and Seymour Epstein from the University of Massachusetts showed participants two bowls filled with different mixes of red and white jellybeans. They then asked the participants to choose which bowl they would like to pick from. If they drew a red jellybean, they would win $1.

The first bowl was smaller with just ten jellybeans, one of which was red. The second, larger bowl had 100 beans in it, eight of which were red. Looking at the odds, the first bowl gave the pickers the best chance of success. However, nearly half of the participants opted for the suboptimal choice.

The psychologists repeated the experiment seven times. Each time they varied the mix of colours in the bowl with 100 beans. It had anywhere between five and nine of the all-important red ones. The ratio in the smaller bowl stayed the same. That meant the odds were always worse in the large bowl.

Across the studies, 82% of the participants picked from the larger bowl at least once. They chose the bowl with the larger absolute number of winning beans, rather than the bowl with the best proportions.

According to the psychologists:

Subjects reported that although they knew the probabilities were against them, they felt they had a better chance when there were more red beans.

They consistently found that subjects focused on the headline number (i.e., the number of red beans, the numerator), rather than the number of times the event could occur (i.e., all the beans, the denominator).

You can make denominator neglect work for you. Here's how.

How can you apply this bias?

1. Applying the rule of 100 to promotions

Experiments about jellybeans might feel a long way from your pressing challenges, but there are commercial applications too. For example, you can harness the finding when you communicate discounts, as shown by an experiment by Eva González from the EGADE Business School in Mexico.

In 2016, she recruited 75 participants and showed them a deal for a pack of balloons normally priced at 48 pesos. Sometimes the participants saw the balloons being discounted by 12 pesos, on other occasions by 25%.

The eagle-eyed mathematicians among you will have noticed that's the same reduction. However, the groups rated the deal differently: those who saw the percentage discount rated it as better. They scored the perceived value at 3.73, whereas those who saw the absolute discount rated it at just 3.46: a drop of 8%.

But that was just the first half of her experiment. Next, González showed a separate group of participants a jacket normally priced at 480 pesos. Some people saw it being discounted by 120 pesos, others by 25%. Again, this is the same reduction.

This time those who saw the absolute discount rated the deal highest. That group scored the deal at 4.16, compared to 3.7 among those exposed to the percentage discount. That's a statistically significant 12% swing in ratings.

González's study found that people put too much emphasis on the headline figure rather than what the number represents. So, they are more likely to think 25% is better than 12 pesos off, because 25 is larger than 12. Just as with the jellybean study, consumers tend to neglect the denominator.

This leads to what Wharton professor Jonah Berger calls the Rule of 100. In his words:

The Rule of 100 says that under 100 percentage discounts seem larger than absolute ones. But over 100, things reverse. Over 100, absolute discounts seem larger than percentage ones.

If your brand is priced at under £100 (or dollars or yen) then communicate the discount using percentages, whereas if you're priced at more than £100 then display the discount in absolute terms.

2. Consider offering multiple stacked discounts

But that's not the only way you can harness denominator neglect. Another approach is to split your discounts, a tactic known as discount stacking.

Let's begin, as ever, with an experiment. This time it's from Akshay Rao from the University of Minnesota and Haipeng Chen from Texas A&M University.

In 2007 the researchers persuaded a store to run a series of discounts on their chopping boards. Sometimes the store offered a straight 40% off, on other occasions they displayed the price reduction in two parts. The discount was described as 20% off, followed by another 25% discount on top of that.

The two discounts are economically identical.[1] So if people behaved like "desiccated calculating machines"[2] the deals should be equally appealing, and sales should be roughly the same in either setting. But that's not what happened. Across a one-month period, sales were significantly higher when the deal was positioned as a double discount.

This deviation from mathematically optimal behaviour can be explained by the principle of denominator neglect. Once again people interpret numbers at face value rather than weigh up what

---

1   Not being the most mathematically literate person, I found this difference hard to believe from first glance. I had to double-check myself a few times. So, if you need to go and find a calculator and check for yourself, please do.
2   A phrase supposedly coined by Nye Bevan, the Labour health secretary, to describe his party leader, Hugh Gaitskell.

they represent. They add up 20% and 25% as 45% and therefore prefer it to a straight 40% off. In their rush to make snap decisions they forget that the second discount is being calculated off a smaller base and therefore is less valuable.

The implication is simple – rather than running simple one-off discounts, test whether a two-tier approach works for you.

3. Present your stacked discounts in ascending order

If you do use stacked discounts, bear in mind the nuances discovered by Han Gong from Shanghai University of Finance and Economics. In 2019 Gong showed participants one of two ads for a $100 sweater. Both ads used discount stacking, however the order in which they applied the discounts varied.

In one version, the sweater was marked down by 10%, with an extra 40% off this amount. In another version, the discounts were reversed: 40% off the original price followed by an extra 10% off.

Gong found that the purchase intent was 15% higher when the discounts were presented in ascending sequence (i.e., 10% followed by an additional 40% off), compared to a descending sequence. In the words of the psychologist:

… we propose that consumers establish a reference for one discount, and compare the additional discount thereto.

In other words, the first number establishes what a reasonable discount looks like. If you start with a large offer, then the smaller follow-up feels miserly. However, if you flip that and begin with a small discount, then the next, bigger offer feels generous.

4. Reframe the discount as a comparison against the sale price

Let's look at one more tactical application. In 2018, Abhijit Guha from the University of South Carolina conducted a study across four grocery stores in Sweden, using a range of household products (shampoo, napkins, coffee and fresh cream).

Guha tested different sales messages. In all cases, the sale sign showed both the original price and the sale price. However, half of these signs emphasised the reduced price, e.g., "now 31% lower", while the others stressed the higher original price, e.g., "was 44% higher".

The psychologist found that sales of the four products more than doubled when the sale framing read "was higher" rather than "now lower".

So, test this tweak on your next promotion. After all, there's no additional cost – you have to frame your discount in one of the two ways so why not test Guha's idea and see if it applies as powerfully to your category.

Applying the idea laterally

The studies we have discussed so far apply the principle of denominator neglect quite literally. They show that across a range of circumstances people tend to react to the number itself rather than what that number represents.

But there's a broader underlying point. These studies show again and again that people react to how deep the discounts feel rather than how deep the discounts are. That principle can be applied more broadly.

5. Adjust the size of fonts when displaying prices to harness magnitude representation congruency

In 2005 Keith Coulter from Clark University and Robin Coulter from the University of Connecticut tested an idea they called 'magnitude representation congruency'. This is the idea that prices written in a larger font are assumed to be pricier than those written in a smaller font. People conflate the font size and the actual cost.

To test their hypothesis, they recruited 65 participants and gave them a booklet with a series of ads. One of the products mentioned was a pair of discounted roller skates. In the control condition, the lower sale price appeared in a larger font than the regular price:

Regular Price: $239.99   Sale Price: $199.99

In the test condition, it was the regular price that appeared larger:

Regular Price: $239.99   Sale Price: $199.99

Participants rated the likelihood of buying the product at 3.63 on a seven-point scale when the sale price was displayed larger than the regular price. However, their likelihood to purchase increased by 25% to 4.54 when the regular price was largest.

This suggests that to increase perceptions of value, the font size of the regular price should be increased so that it's larger than the sale price.

The Coulter study is interesting, but you might be nervous about the sample size. It was only 65 people after all. So before applying this experiment you might want to run one of your own to see whether the results hold in your category. But before you rush off to put a test in place, why not read the next chapter. It has a few bits of advice on running tests...

REFERENCES

'Conflict between intuitive and rational processing: When people behave against their better judgment' by Veronika Denes-Raj and Seymour Epstein [*Journal of Personality and Social Psychology*, Vol, 66, No. 5, pp. 819–829, 1994]

'Amount off vs percentage off – when does it matter?' by Eva Gonzáles, Eduardo Esteva, Anne L. Roggeveen and Dhruv Grewal [*Journal of Business Research*, Vol. 69, No. 3, pp. 1022–1027, 2016]

'When Two Plus Two Is Not Equal to Four: Errors in Processing Multiple Percentage Changes' by Akshay Rao and Haipeng Chen [*Journal of Consumer Research*, Vol. 34, No. 3, pp. 327–340, 2007]

'The Illusion of Double-Discount: Using Reference Points in Promotion Framing' by Han Gong, Jianxiong Huang and Kim Huat Goh [*Journal of Consumer Psychology*, Vol. 29, No. 3, pp. 483–491, 2019]

'Reframing the Discount as a Comparison against the Sale Price: Does it Make the Discount More Attractive?' by Abhijit Guha, Abhijit Biswas, Dhruv Grewal, Swati Verma, Somak Banerjee and Jens Nordfält [*Journal of Marketing Research*, Vol. 55, No. 3, pp. 339–351, 2016]

'Size Does Matter: The Effects of Magnitude Representation Congruency on Price Perceptions and Purchase Likelihood' by Keith Coulter and Robin Coulter [*Journal of Consumer Psychology*, Vol. 15, No. 1, pp. 64–76, 2005]

9

THE NEED TO
EXPERIMENT

YOU HEAR A clatter at the office front door. When you investigate, there's a handful of letters and leaflets on the doormat. Something bright red stands out from the white and brown envelopes. You peer closer.

It's an envelope from Christian Aid asking for a donation, which they'll come and collect in a week's time.

You put your hand into your pocket and stuff a crumpled fiver into the envelope.

WHAT MADE YOU donate? Was it the copy, the image they used or something that you can't even verbalise? Let's look at an experiment that might offer an explanation.

Each May, Christian Aid volunteers hand deliver seven million envelopes to British houses and then return later to collect them along with any donations. In 2018 they decided to apply behavioural science to their messaging to boost donations.

Working with Ogilvy Consulting they tested seven messages across 1.2 million envelopes. These can be seen in the following table.

Bias	Message
Control	Simple donation request
Labour illusion	"Hand Delivered, Hand Collected, by your local volunteer" stamp
Scarcity	"We're collecting donations this week only!" banner
Cognitive ease	"Appeal. Donation Envelope" banner
Affordance cues	Portrait orientation envelope to give cues that it was an envelope rather than a leaflet
Salience	Highlighting the benefits of Gift Aid "Boost your donation by 25% for free"
Costly signalling	Using thicker paper stock to increase the perceived value of the envelope

Have a read of the messages and then pick which two you think were the least effective in terms of total revenue generated.

Done? In that case turn over the page to see the results.

Bias	Strategy	Average donation
Control	Simple donation request	£0.34
Labour illusion	"Hand Delivered, Hand Collected, by your local volunteer" stamp	£0.39
Scarcity	"We're collecting donations this week only!" banner	£0.28
Cognitive ease	"Appeal. Donation Envelope" banner	£0.38
Affordance cues	Portrait orientation envelope to give cues that it was an envelope rather than a leaflet	£0.40
Salience	Highlighting the benefits of Gift Aid "Boost your donation by 25% for free"	£0.18
Costly signalling	Using thicker paper stock to increase the perceived value of the envelope	£0.39

How did you do? If you predicted the results correctly perhaps you don't need this chapter;[1] but for the rest of us, it's worth contemplating the results.

The worst two performers, designed to elicit the biases of salience and scarcity, backfired and actually generated less money than the control.[2] The Ogilvy team hypothesised that perhaps the time

---

1 Actually, you do.
2 Ogilvy Consulting produce an annual report which outlines their recent work. It includes both the agency's successes and failures, which is something to be admired.

urgency of the scarcity message "gave people a justification not to donate". They also wondered if Gift Aid reduced donations since it "made donating too transactional" (crowding out the 'warm glow' of donation). These are plausible explanations, but they're easy to make after you know the results, hard to identify beforehand.

When I've shown people these messages, few can pick the worst performers. This should give us pause for thought. If we struggle to reliably predict the impact of our interventions, then it means we should proceed with a degree of caution. We need to test. This shouldn't be seen as a failure of knowledge but a recognition of the complexity of people and the context-dependent nature of behaviour.

> If we struggle to reliably predict the impact of our interventions, then we should proceed with a degree of caution.

Let's look at how experimentation can help you.

How can you apply this bias?

1. Be more sceptical about claimed data

Once you have decided to create a test, the next question is how to structure it. The main rule is not to trust people's claims. One of the broad themes in behavioural science is that what people *say* motivates them and what *actually* motivates them are two different things.

Sometimes this is because people lie when they are questioned. Even more problematically, people often don't know their genuine motivations. People are, in the words of Timothy Wilson, professor at the University of Virginia, "Strangers to themselves".

That's not an empty claim.

The idea that people don't know their own motivations is demonstrated by a 1999 experiment led by Adrian North, then a psychologist at Leicester University.

Over a fortnight he alternated the background music played in a supermarket wine aisle, between traditional German oompah music and French accordion music. When accordion music was played, French wine accounted for 83% of wine sales; when the soundtrack was oompah music, German wine represented 65% of sales. The scale of the variation shows that music was the prime determinant of the type of wine bought.

Later, as shoppers were leaving the supermarket, North stopped them and asked if they had bought any French or German wine. If they had, he asked them why they had bought that particular bottle. Only 2% of buyers spontaneously attributed their choice to the music. Even when prompted, 86% of people stated that it had no impact at all. People's claims about their motivations were at complete odds with reality.

It's not that they were lying; more that people were unaware of their genuine motivations.

Findings like North's suggest that you should treat any results from surveys and focus groups with a healthy scepticism.

So, if you're not going to use claimed data what should you do? Well, behavioural scientists prioritise observed data.

There are two techniques in particular that can help you in this area: monadic testing and field experiments.

2. Improve your surveys by using monadic testing

Monadic tests are a simple way of generating more accurate answers from surveys. The approach involves randomly splitting the participants into groups or cells. Each cell is told about the same outline of a concept. However, each cell has an additional fact woven into the summary, and that fact varies between cells. Afterwards, we question the respondents as to how they feel about the concept. Any difference in ratings is attributed to the changing variable.

If that sounds a bit confusing, a concrete example should help. Let's look at the research I did on temporal reframing – the idea that when weighing up a price, people overemphasise the sum quoted and place too little weight on the time frame.

I showed 500 people a picture of a car and a brief description. That was the same for everyone. But some participants saw the price conveyed as £4.57 a day, some as £32 a week, some as £139 a month and the final group as £1,668 a year. If you do the maths, all four prices were the same over an entire year.

Finally, the participants were asked to rate the value of the car. The results revealed that the longer the time frame, the less appealing the deal. When the prices were shown as a daily figure, they were four times more likely to be rated as a great deal than when they were shown as an annual amount.

The implication for businesses is simple – make sure you convey your price in the smallest possible units of time.

However, it's the technique, rather than the finding, that's most relevant. The oblique approach of monadic testing leads to more accurate answers. If you asked people directly 'Which price would most effectively persuade you the car was good value, £1 a day or £7 a week?' they would be nonplussed. They would tell you that they're exactly the same. But by questioning people indirectly, monadic testing flushes out the genuine motivations for behaviour that people might not be aware of.

Next time you run a survey, make sure you use this simple technique.

3. Complement monadic tests
with field experiments

Monadic testing is useful, but there's still an element of claimed data. An even better approach is to run a field experiment. This is one of the standard approaches used by psychologists.

The technique is simple. You create two scenarios in a naturalistic setting – so not a survey – where all factors are kept the same except for one. You then measure the differences in behaviour in those settings. Any disparity in behaviour can be attributed to the changed variable.

Again, if that sounds a little abstract, let's look at an example of a field experiment I ran a few years ago when I was working with a major British supermarket who wanted to overturn a misperception that they were expensive.

After looking at their promotional ads I noticed that they rarely used charm pricing. This is the practice of setting prices to end in nine, on the basis that they are seen as better value than other prices.[3] I suggested they ensure more of their prices, both in store and in the ads, were charm prices.

The client wasn't convinced. They believed prices ending in nine were tacky and might damage their hard-earned reputation for quality. That's not an unreasonable belief. There's some evidence that

---

3   If you're interested in charm pricing, I cover some of the evidence in *The Choice Factory*. For example, a 2003 study by Eric Anderson, from the University of Chicago, and Duncan Simester, from MIT. They partnered with a mail-order retailer to test the impact of different prices on the sales of dresses. When priced at $34 they sold 16 dresses, at $39 they sold 21 while at $44 they shifted 17. Since the sample sizes were small, they repeated the experiment – each time they found the same result. The psychologists argued that through constant repetition, steep discounting and charm pricing have become intertwined. The mere sight of 99p denotes a bargain, regardless of the underlying value.

shoppers prefer round prices. In 2013 Michael Lynn from Cornell University analysed sales at a self-service petrol station in upstate New York. He found that 56% of sales ended in .00. That's far higher than chance alone. Lynn suggested that reflects drivers' preference for round prices.

But a preference for round numbers in petrol stations is a long way from proving that charm prices degrade value in supermarkets. This uncertainty meant that it was the perfect moment for a test. Unfortunately, the brand wasn't prepared to provide the necessary funds for a major project, so Alex Boyd and I designed a simple, low-cost study.

We asked shoppers on a busy London street to sample some chocolate. The food came with a backstory – we told them it was a brand of chocolate called Bolivar, that it was launching soon in the UK and what the cost would be. We told some people it would be 79p for a small bar and others that it would be 80p.

The part about it being Bolivar chocolate was a bit of harmless subterfuge. In reality the samples came from broken up Dairy Milks. But we created this cover story so that people didn't have preconceptions about the brand which might have drowned out any impact of the price.

After the shoppers had sampled the chocolate, we asked them to rate the taste on a scale of 1–10. The shoppers who thought the bar cost 80p rated it at 7.1, whereas those who thought it cost 79p rated it slightly higher at 7.6 – a statistically insignificant difference.

For less than £20 and a couple of afternoons of work we had tested the hypothesis and shown that charm prices, at least in the world of chocolate bars, don't degrade quality perceptions.

So, you now have two techniques at your disposal. Field experiments have a greater degree of realism so I would prioritise them over monadic testing. But there might be times when you need a quick answer, in which case the simplicity of a monadic test is ideal.

4. Follow a six-step process

Now you know a couple of useful techniques let's run through the process you should follow when you want to run an experiment. There are six key steps:

Step 1 – *identify the specific problem you're trying to solve.* This should be a tangible issue. Don't just define the challenge as 'more sales' or 'boosting profit'. That's too vague. Instead, split that broader aim into smaller, specific problems you need to overcome. In the supermarket example I mentioned, this was determining whether charm prices damaged quality perceptions.

Step 2 – *run through the existing research findings on the topic.* There are thousands of academic studies about how to change behaviour. Look through these to see if the challenge that you're facing has already been studied.

In the supermarket example, the study that supported the idea that charm prices might be damaging to quality perceptions was the one by Lynn.

Step 3 – *decide whether the existing research is satisfactory. Once you have conducted the literature review then decide whether the existing research answers your question adequately.*

That's often not the case. Sometimes the sample in the academic study is unrepresentative, sometimes the experiment was conducted in a different market or category to yours or sometimes there are issues with the experimental design.

In our field experiment example, we had the issue that the existing study looked at preference rather than any impact on quality perceptions. Because of that we needed to move to step 4.

Step 4 – *design your own field experiment or monadic test.* Remember to make sure:

1. You keep it simple. Stick to testing one thing at a time. Some of my early experiments unraveled when I tried to test multiple metrics at once.

2. The sample is representative – that is, the participants reflect the audience you're interested in.

3. The participants don't know why they're taking part in an experiment – otherwise, their behaviour might be affected.

4. You keep all variables the same in the two scenarios – apart from one.

5. The sample is large enough that the findings are statistically significant.

Follow these simple steps and the experiment doesn't have to cost much. In fact, it's much better if it doesn't. If you follow a fast and frugal approach to insight, then you can run tests every week. That's far better than running a really expensive piece of research just once a year.

Think of this step as hypothesis testing – you don't need everything to be perfect. Just an improvement on the existing work.

Step 5 – *run a real-world test.* Once you have run your fast and frugal experiment then run a larger real-world experiment. So, in the case of the monadic test we discussed, the next step would be to run an A/B test on your website. The majority of visitors would see the price in the time unit you normally display – that's the control – whereas a proportion would see the weekly or daily price. You would then monitor the sales rate in the different conditions.

Step 6 – *change your communications as per the findings!* An obvious but important point. There's no benefit in running these experiments and finding a relevant result unless you change your behaviour afterwards.

If all this discussion of experiments has got you thinking about what study you're going to run, then how about conducting one into the principle of framing? If you're not familiar with this bias then you're in luck, just turn to the next page and I'll tell you everything you need to know...

REFERENCES

The Behavioural Science Annual 2018–2019 by Ogilvy Change [2019] retrieved from:
www.ogilvyconsulting.com/wp-content/uploads/2019/07/Ogilvy-TheAnnual.pdf

'The influence of in-store music on wine selections' by Adrian North, David Hargreaves and Jennifer McKendrick [*Journal of Applied Psychology*, Vol. 84, No. 2, 1999]

'Do consumers prefer round prices? Evidence from pay what-you-want decisions and self-pumped gasoline purchases' by Michael Lynn, Sean Masaki Flynn and Chelsea Helion [*Journal of Economic Psychology*, Vol. 36, pp. 96–102, 2013]

10

FRAMING

IT'S YOUR FRIEND Hope's birthday in a few weeks, so you nip out of work and head to the high street to find a present. At the local jewellers you see a Victorian brooch that you know she'll love.

You hold your breath as you turn over the price label ready for an uncomfortable shock.

You're pleasantly surprised. The price is less than expected. Beaming, you head to the cashier.

While standing in line you spot a small handwritten sign stuck to the till. In a scrawl it says, "Surcharge for credit cards of 2.5%".

You don't have enough cash to pay for the brooch. You'll have to fork out extra money for the privilege of paying by card. Your cheeks flush.

THE SHOPKEEPER COULD have avoided irritating you by increasing the base prices by 2.5% and then offering an equally sized cash discount. While an economist might argue that the situations are identical, a psychologist would recognise that they frame the situation differently. Since losses loom larger than gains, shoppers are comfortable using their cards and forgoing a discount, whereas paying a surcharge for cash would have been too painful.

That's not mere conjecture. A 2000 study commissioned by the EU of 150 cardholders in the Netherlands found that 74% regarded credit card surcharges as bad, but that figure dropped to 49% when the situation was framed as a cash discount.

The idea that a simple twist in language can radically alter the impact of a situation extends beyond payment means. A classic demonstration comes from a 1988 experiment by Irwin Levin and Gary Gaeth at the University of Iowa. They served a batch of minced beef to students, sometimes telling them it was "75% lean" and sometimes, "25% fat".

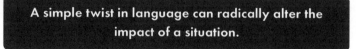

A simple twist in language can radically alter the impact of a situation.

Even though the beef in both scenarios was identical – it came from the same batch – and the information about fat levels was objectively the same, the frame affected their taste ratings.

The researchers found that students preferred the mince when they were told it was 75% lean. They rated the quality and leanness 19% and 31% higher respectively than that of the 25% fat mince.

But why is framing so important?

The reason why framing has such an effect is discussed in *Thinking, Fast and Slow* by Daniel Kahneman. He explored the idea that we make decisions based on the "known knowns". That is, we consider only the information before us – ignoring potentially relevant factors we cannot perceive at that moment. It's a concept that he terms 'What You See Is All There Is' or, as he abbreviates it, WYSIATI.

In Kahneman's words:

WYSIATI means that we use the information we have as if it is the only information. We don't spend much time saying, "Well, there is much we don't know."We make do with what we do know. And that concept is very central to the functioning of our mind.

It's an intriguing idea for a marketer. It means you can shape a consumer's emotional reaction by editing the focus of their attention.

But it's more than framing that matters. A single word can make a difference. A stark demonstration can be seen in the 1974 research of Elizabeth Loftus and John Palmer at the University of Washington. They showed participants a video of a car accident and then asked them to estimate how fast the cars were travelling.

However, the question was altered by one word – the verb – between participants. Specifically, they were asked: "About how fast were the cars going when they (smashed/collided/bumped/hit/contacted) each other?"

This single change had a significant impact on their estimations of the speed. Participants who were asked the 'smashed' question thought the cars were travelling 27% faster than those who were asked the 'contacted' question.

Verb	Participants' estimates of the speed (mph)
Smashed	40.8
Collided	39.8
Bumped	38.1
Hit	34.0
Contacted	31.8

Results from Loftus and Palmer's 1974 study.

The verb in the question acted like a lens that distorted the way participants viewed reality.

The power of language to shape our perceptions isn't limited to the lab. A Machiavellian motoring example dates back to 1920s America, when the proliferation of cars resulted in a growing number of pedestrian fatalities. Unsurprisingly, this resulted in public anger towards the auto manufacturers.

In an attempt to swing the blame away from drivers, the manufacturers banded together and coined a new word – "jaywalking" – to describe the previously uncontentious act of crossing the road.

At the time, a 'jay' was a derogatory word: an out-of-towner, an unsophisticated hick, confused by the rules of the city. So to be caught jaywalking was shaming. The word caught on, and the responsibility for deaths shifted from drivers to walkers. In fact, jaywalkers are still fined in US cities today.

It's not just 1920s America where you can see the impact of a well-chosen word. A more recent example comes from London in 2012 as covered in the excellent *How Not to Plan* by Sarah Carter and Les Binet.

Danny Boyle, the director of films such as *Slumdog Millionaire* and *Trainspotting*, was responsible for creating the opening ceremony for the Olympics. He had organised a dress rehearsal of the show to be run live in front of an audience of 60,000.

While the presence of an audience boosted the realism and prepared the actors, it created another problem: how do you stop the audience from revealing any spoilers? Boyle refrained from asking the audience to keep the details of the ceremony secret. Instead he asked them to "save the surprise". It's a subtle shift that emphasises passing on details is not the sharing of precious knowledge, but tarnishing the excitement of the show.

Boyle's choice of words proved to be effective with remarkably few of the surprises on the opening night being leaked to the media.

So, the message here is clear. Choose your words wisely: they have the power to change behaviour.

Let's look at how you can do just that.

How can you apply this bias?

While it's important to know that subtle shifts in language can change the impact of a proposal, that's quite broad advice. Here are three specific ways in which you can harness the power of framing.

1. Focus on losses, rather than gains

Perhaps the simplest application is to consider focusing on losses rather than gains when promoting your product. This taps into the idea of loss aversion, discovered by the Israeli psychologists Amos Tversky and Daniel Kahneman, which suggests that losses loom larger than gains.

Supporting evidence comes from a simple experiment by the Harvard psychologist Elliot Aronson.[1] In 1988 Aronson approached 404 homeowners and told them about the impact of insulating their homes. Half were told that if they insulated their homes, they would be able to save 75 cents a day, whereas the others were told that if they failed to insulate their homes, they would lose the same amount.

---

1   Aronson is probably best known for the discovery of the 'pratfall effect'. This is the idea that people or products who exhibit a flaw become more popular. It's the idea behind many of the greatest ad campaigns: VW (Ugly is only skin deep), Marmite (You either love it or hate it), Guinness (Good things come to those who wait). You can read more in my first book, *The Choice Factory*.

THE ILLUSION OF CHOICE

Aronson then asked them if they would like to sign up for more information on an insulation service. When told how much money they could gain by insulating their house, 39% of homeowners requested more information. However, 61% of those told how much they stood to lose from inadequate insulation signed up. That's a 56% improvement in sign-up rates.

This finding is easy for marketers to apply. Most campaigns focus on what you will gain by buying a brand. Loss aversion suggests a subtle shift: instead focus on what people will miss out on if they don't switch.

So, imagine you work on a phone brand. You could apply this idea by tweaking your copy to say, 'switch to us or you'll lose out on £30 a month', rather than mimicking what most marketers do: telling customers they could gain that amount of money.

2. The benefits of using nouns rather than verbs

There's another simple copy tweak you can make to more effectively change behaviour: consider shifting from using verbs to nouns. In 2011 Christopher Bryan at Stanford University recruited Californians who were eligible to vote in the 2008 presidential election but had not yet registered.

Participants were asked to complete surveys about their intention to vote. Each participant completed one of two versions. In the first version, a short series of questions referred to voting using a noun. For example, "How important is it to you to be a voter in the upcoming election?" In the other version, the questions referred to voting using a verb. For example, "How important is it to you to vote in the upcoming election?"

After completing the surveys the participants were informed that to vote they would need to register. Bryan found that those in the noun group were significantly more interested in registering to vote than the others.

In the words of the psychologist:

Noun wording leads people to see attributes as more representative of a person's essential qualities.

In other words, verbs represent what we do, nouns reflect what we are. And it's the latter that has the greater persuasive power.

If you want to encourage people to identify with their past behaviour, then use nouns. For example, a while ago I worked with a magazine brand who wanted to encourage people to renew their subscriptions. We adapted the language used in their renewal letters from "thank you for subscribing" to "thank you for being a subscriber". A small but powerful tweak.

3. Harness social proof to minimise irritation with shortages

Finally, let's consider how a subtle shift in language can reduce customer irritation when your stocks are running low. In 2019 Robert Peterson, from the University of Texas showed 1,117 participants a product page on a website. The product was either labelled "Out-of-Stock", "Sold Out" or "Unavailable".

Even though all other details on the page were consistent, the label used significantly affected the reaction of the respondent. The term "sold out" produced significantly fewer negative reactions than the other two labels: respondents felt 8% less disappointment compared to when the product was framed as "out-of-stock" and 15% less disappointment compared to when it was framed as "unavailable".

"Sold out" may be more effective because it emphasises the

popularity of the product, thereby tapping into social proof, whereas "unavailable" hints that there has been a logistical issue.[2]

In this chapter we've discussed three specific ways to harness subtle shifts in language: loss aversion, the power of nouns and social proof.

However, remember back to the incident with the cash surcharge at the beginning of the chapter. That involved another element of framing. The way the charge was described made it feel unfair: why should you get charged more for paying by credit card?

Fairness is a surprisingly powerful driver of behaviour. In the next chapter we'll discuss how you can turn that insight to your advantage...

REFERENCES

'How consumers are affected by the framing of attribute information before and after consuming the product' by Irwin Levin and Gary Gaeth [*Journal of Consumer Research*, Vol. 15, No. 3, pp. 374–378, 1998]

'Reconstruction of automobile destruction: An example of the interaction between language and memory' by Elizabeth Loftus and John Palmer [*Journal of Verbal Learning & Verbal Behavior*, Vol. 13, No. 5, pp. 585–589, 1974]

'Using social cognition and persuasion to promote energy conservation: A quasi-experiment' by Marti Hope Gonzales, Elliot Aronson and Mark A. Costanzo [*Journal of Applied Social Psychology*, Vol. 18, No. 12, Pt 2, pp. 1049–1066, 1988]

'Motivating voter turnout by invoking the self' by Christopher Bryan, Gregory Walton, Todd Rogers and Carol Dweck [*Proceedings of the National Academy of Sciences of the United States of America*, Vol. 108, No. 31, pp. 12653–12656, 2011]

'Out-of-stock, sold out, or unavailable? Framing a product outage in online retailing' by Robert Peterson, Yeolib Kim and Jaeseok Jeong [*Marketing Letters*, Vol. 37, No. 3, pp. 428–440, 2019]

---

2   Social proof is the idea that if you make a behaviour or product appear popular it will become more appealing. You can read more about this concept in my book *The Choice Factory*.

11

FAIRNESS

WHEN YOU RETURN from your trip to the jewellers there's an email from your boss waiting for you. You open it excitedly, as you have been waiting for news on a potential bonus.

It's good news. You've been rewarded with £1,000 for all your hard efforts this year. You exhale loudly; it's considerably more than you were hoping for.

As you turn to your colleague Tom, you blurt out the good news. He congratulates you warmly before adding that he's looking forward to spending his £1,100 bonus on a long-haul trip.

You struggle to maintain your smile. How has Tom been awarded more; you both do the same job? Your thoughts turn to a recent meeting with a recruitment consultant, maybe that other agency wouldn't be such a bad place after all...

YOUR REACTION MIGHT seem strange from a purely logical perspective.

Why does it matter what others are paid? Surely, it's the absolute amount of your bonus that is most important? After all, £1,000 buys the same amount of goods regardless of what your colleague has been given.

Maybe that's how people *should* behave, but it's not how they *do* behave. And it's the latter point that is of interest to us.

When it comes to actual behaviour, we see repeatedly that fairness transgressions motivate people to action.

The first experiments on this topic stretch back to 1982 and the work of Werner Güth, Rolf Schmittberger and Bernd Schwarze from the University of Cologne. The trio designed a test called the ultimatum game. This involved recruiting pairs of people, with one participant given the role of the proposer, the other the receiver.

The proposer was given a sum of money – in the original experiment somewhere between four and ten Deutschmarks (around £4 to £10 in today's money) – and told to split the cash with the receiver as they deemed fit. The receiver – who was kept separate from the proposer – was given just two options. They could accept the offer without negotiation, or they could reject it, in which case both parties received nothing.

Prior to this experiment, most economists believed that receivers would accept an uneven split, say two of the ten marks. After all, they were better off if they agreed.

But that's not what happened.

When proposers offered grossly unfair splits – say, keeping 80% of the cash for themselves – most receivers rejected the deal. People were prepared to punish the transgressor, even at a cost to themselves.

> People are prepared to punish someone who transgresses the concept of fairness, even at a cost to themselves.

You will have noted that these are quite small sums and perhaps this suggests that the finding only holds with trivial amounts of cash. However, in 1999 Lisa Cameron from the University of Melbourne reran the ultimatum game in Indonesia and set the stakes much higher. The amount split went up to $100. Even when the sums equated to three times the monthly expenditure of participants, grossly unfair splits were still rejected by the receiver.

That might appear puzzling, but this behaviour has an evolutionary benefit. Humans are only powerful when we band together in groups. And, if a group is going to operate efficiently it needs to resolve the freeloader problem. Going to great lengths – even at a cost to ourselves – to punish those who transgress fairness norms is one way of doing that.

A long pedigree

The importance of fairness stretches beyond even our human ancestors. You can see it in primates.

In 2003 Frans de Waal and Susan Brosnan from Emory University trained capuchin monkeys to hand over a pebble to them in exchange for a cucumber slice.

The researchers then placed a second monkey into an adjacent Perspex cage. The transparent setting meant the animals were able to monitor each other. At first, the experiment continued in the same manner – the monkeys handed over a stone and they received their reward.

But then the psychologists mixed things up. They rewarded one monkey with cucumber, the other with grapes. This introduced an element of unfairness as monkeys strongly prefer grapes. In the words of de Waal, "the food preferences of my capuchin monkeys correspond exactly with the prices in the supermarket."

Even though the absolute benefit to the monkey hadn't changed,

THE ILLUSION OF CHOICE

those being paid in cucumbers rebelled. When they saw their partner receiving a grape, they rejected the proffered cucumber about half the time – often hurling the offending item out of the cage in disgust.[1] This behaviour is out of character – in the original experiment, which was set up to be fair because all monkeys received cucumbers, the monkeys rejected their payment only 5% of the time.

These results are fascinating as it is millions of years since monkeys and humans shared a common ancestor. If this reaction to unfairness is found in both species, it suggests it has deep roots, and it's one we should harness when trying to influence behaviour.

From cucumbers to cash

While these experiments demonstrate the depth of feelings that unfairness generates, the settings they were conducted in are a long way from commerce. With that in mind, in 2020 I ran an experiment to see if these findings might be relevant in business.

I told a group of British respondents about a supermarket that had raised the price of a pack of nine toilet rolls from £5 to £6 during the early stages of the Covid-19 pandemic. Many economists might feel this is legitimate, simply reflecting supply and demand. However, that's not how most customers interpreted it: 83% of respondents, the overwhelming majority, found the price rise unfair. Brits weren't alone. I reran the survey in France and the negative responses were even more pronounced, with 96% of respondents judging the price rise unfair.

This experiment suggests that people are attuned to matters of fairness when shopping. However, being aware of an issue and

---

1   My description of this experiment doesn't do it justice. You can watch de Waal's TED talk in which he includes footage of the aggrieved monkeys here: www.youtube.com/watch?v=meiU6TxysCg.

changing your behaviour based on it are two different things. It's easy to take umbrage at a thought experiment when there's no money at stake. Would consumers be so principled if cash was involved?

An experiment from Sally Blount from the University of Chicago and Max Bazerman from Northwestern University looked into just that. The researchers offered 126 students a small payment to participate in an experiment on political decision-making. However, the political study was a ruse – what the academics were really interested in was how many people agreed to take part.

They approached each student with one of two offers. The first batch of students were offered $7 to participate. In that scenario 72% – nearly three-quarters – agreed.

Others were offered $8 to take part, but they were told a harmless lie: that previous subjects had been paid $10. Even though these participants were offered $1 more than the first group, a lower proportion agreed to take part: only 54%. That's a 25% reduction.

Participants didn't just weigh up their absolute payment when deciding whether to take part – they were also motivated by the comparative amount. They were prepared to turn down a profitable opportunity rather than be treated unfairly. Blount's experiment gives us the strongest proof yet that perceptions of fairness shape commercial behaviour.

Let's look at how to apply this effect.

How can you apply this bias?

1. Harness righteous indignation

The first implication of these experiments is to harness the righteous indignation generated by fairness transgressions. Persuading someone to switch brands and trial your product can be difficult. But if you can target potential customers after their existing provider has behaved unfairly then those bonds of inertia will be weakened.

Consider banking. If you're promoting current account switching, the ideal moment is to target a rival bank's customers just after they have been hit by a disproportionate penalty. Say, being charged £10 for barely going over their overdraft limit.

Or better still, consider reframing your competition's behaviour as unfair. So, a new taxi brand might identify Uber's surge pricing as a potential weak spot and instead emphasise their own flat-fee approach.

Surge pricing certainly feels like an opportunity. In 2015 Jenny Riddell and I contacted 367 people on the day of a Tube strike and asked them about the fairness of Uber's surge pricing: 83% thought the price increase was unfair. In fact, when we probed further, they described the policy as "disgusting", "taking advantage" and "profiteering".

2. Apply the principle of fairness to your pricing

Second, consider applying these principles of fairness to your own pricing. Begin by recognising that what might seem an uncontroversial price rise from your perspective, might be deemed unfair by the customer.

There are experiments that suggest tactics to minimise this risk. The first comes from Richard Thaler, Daniel Kahneman and Jack Knetsch. In 1986 the trio told participants about a range of scenarios in which retailers had increased their prices. For example, a hardware store had increased the prices of their shovels from $15 to $20 the day after a snowstorm. That was rated as unfair by 82% of the participants. Raising prices in the face of greater customer need was interpreted as exploitative.

The academics then explored how this type of price rise could be communicated in a way that diffused the anger. They gave participants another scenario:

Suppose that, due to a transportation mix-up, there is a local shortage of lettuce and the wholesale price has increased. A local grocer has bought the usual quantity of lettuce at a price that is 30 cents per head higher than normal. The grocer raises the price of lettuce to customers by 30 cents per head.

In this scenario, only 21% of participants thought that this price rise was unacceptable. The implication is clear: if you're raising your price, provide a justification. Have you had increases in terms of wages, taxes or raw materials? If so, tell your customers. Too many brands fail to mention these price factors. Instead, be explicit about your predicament, and customers are more likely to accept the increase.

3. Harness the power of because

Often brands shy away from explaining the rationale for price rises as they fear the justification isn't impressive enough. However, a study by the Harvard psychologist Ellen Langer suggests that's a mistake.

In 1978 Langer ran a test at a busy college photocopier. She tried to push into the queues for the machine with one of two requests. The first request was, "Excuse me, I have five pages. May I use the Xerox machine?" In this scenario 60% complied.

Later she approached other people with a subtly modified plea, "Excuse me, I have five pages. May I use the Xerox machine, because I have to make copies?" Note that she's not giving a meaningful reason why she needs to jump the queue. Of course she wants copies, why else would she be using the machine?

However, in the second scenario compliance increased to 93%. Langer argued that even useless, or in her words 'placebic', information boosts compliance if the term 'because' is used. That's due to the fact that the word 'because' is normally followed by a sensible reason. The word itself, devoid of any meaningful rationale, boosted compliance through association.

The lesson from this study is a simple one to apply: always provide a 'because' in your communications.

4. A more lateral interpretation

There's another angle on this tactic that can be applied to price justification. Again, it comes from Thaler. In 1985 he gave each of his participants one of two scenarios. The first went as follows:

> You are lying on the beach on a hot day. All you have to drink is ice water. For the last hour, you have been thinking about how much you would enjoy a nice cold bottle of your favourite brand of beer. A companion gets up to go make a phone call and offers to bring back a beer from the only nearby place where beer is sold, a small, run-down grocery store. He says that the beer might be expensive and so asks how much you are willing to pay for the beer. He says that he will buy the beer if it costs as much or less than the price you state. But if it costs more than the price you state he will not buy it. You trust your friend, and there is no possibility of bargaining with the store owner. What price do you tell him?

The average price cap in this scenario was $1.50. Remember that figure.

The next set of participants were given a similar script with just one change. This time they were told the nearby bar was in a fancy resort hotel. Again, they were asked to state the maximum amount they were willing to pay. This time the average was $2.65.

Remember, the two groups are buying exactly the same commodity – a beer drunk on a beach – and they're stating the maximum they're willing to pay. Despite that, the figure rises by 77% in the second scenario.

Why?

In the context of the experiments that we have listed, I would argue it is partly driven by fairness. If people realise that your brand has higher costs they'll be prepared to pay more. This experiment suggests that you don't have to explicitly state those costs like in Thaler, Kahneman and Knetsch's lettuce scenario, but that you can convey them implicitly.

5. Make sure your customers behave fairly

What about a slightly different challenge? What if your brand needs to ensure that your customers behave fairly? One tactic you can harness is the 'watching eyes effect'.

The academic most associated with this idea is Melissa Bateson of Newcastle University. In 2011 she placed a series of posters in the university's self-clearing cafeteria.

Sometimes the poster contained a pair of eyes with either the message "Please place your trays in the racks provided after you have finished your meal. Thank you" or "Please only consume food and drink purchased on these premises. Thank you". At other times, the eyes were replaced with a picture of flowers.

The researchers then monitored the proportion failing to comply with each of these requests.

Bateson found that the odds of people littering in the presence of posters with eyes fell by around 50%, compared to the posters featuring flowers. This effect occurred irrespective of whether the poster contained an anti-littering message or not. It was the presence of eyes that mattered.

This finding might sound surprising, but it has been supported by a meta-analysis of 15 studies led by Keith Dear from Oxford University. These studies looked at a range of antisocial behaviours, such as littering, bicycle theft and engine idling. Across all these settings Dear found a consistent pattern: when people were in the presence of images of eyes, antisocial behaviour was reduced by up to 35%.

It seems that the presence of eyes reminds us that we might be being watched and that encourages us to behave in a way that society expects. That reduces the likelihood that we will behave unfairly.

We've covered many elements of fairness in this chapter. But there's one related area we've not touched on: how people feel aggrieved if their freedom of choice is removed. That strikes them as unfair. And it's the topic for the next chapter...

REFERENCES

'An experimental analysis of ultimatum bargaining' by Werner Guth, Rolf Schmittberger and Bernd Schwarze [*Journal of Economic Behaviour & Organisation*, Vol. 3, No. 4, pp. 367–388, 1982]

'Raising the stakes in the ultimatum game: Experimental evidence from Indonesia' by Lisa Cameron [*Economic Enquiry*, Vol. 37, No. 1, pp.47–59, 1999]

'Monkeys reject unequal pay' by Frans de Waal and Susan Brosnan [*Nature*, Vol. 425, No. 6955, pp. 297–299, 2003]

'The inconsistent evaluation of absolute versus comparative payoffs in labor supply and bargaining' by Sally Blount and Max Bazerman [*Journal of Economic Behaviour & Organisation*, Vol. 30, No. 2, pp. 227–240, 1996]

'Fairness as a Constraint on Profit Seeking: Entitlements in the Market' by Daniel Kahneman, Jack L. Knetsch and Richard Thaler [*The American Economic Review*, Vol. 76, No. 4, pp. 728–741, 1986]

'The mindlessness of ostensibly thoughtful action: The role of "placebic" information in interpersonal interaction' by Ellen Langer, Arthur Blank and Benzion Chanowitz [*Journal of Personality and Social Psychology*, Vol. 36, No. 6, pp. 635–642, 1978]

'Mental Accounting and Consumer Choice' by Richard Thaler [*Marketing Science*, Vol. 4, No. 3, pp. 199–214, 1985]

'Effects of eye images on everyday cooperative behaviour: A field experiment' by Max Earnest Jones, Melissa Bateson and Daniel Nettle [*Evolution and Human Behaviour*, Vol. 32, No. 3, pp. 172–178, 2011]

'Do "watching eyes" influence antisocial behaviour? A systematic review & meta-analysis' by Keith Dear, Kevin Dutton and Elaine Fox [*Evolution and Human Behaviour*, Vol. 40, No. 3, pp. 269–280, 2019]

12

FREEDOM OF CHOICE

AS YOU PLOUGH through your workload, you're interrupted by a phone call from your partner. They've just got home from work and found the house is a tip.

In their words your daughter's room looks like a bomb has hit it. Clothes are strewn across every surface.

You let out a groan of frustration. Only last night you harangued your daughter for at least ten minutes on the need – no, the absolute necessity – to keep her room tidy. Why has she ignored you?

YOUR ATTEMPT TO influence your child has backfired. By ordering her to comply in a dictatorial manner you inadvertently triggered a psychological bias known as reactance.

This finding was first reported by the Yale psychologist Jack Brehm in 1966. He argued that if people feel their autonomy is threatened, they often react by reasserting their freedom. This means that overly forceful demands are often counterproductive.

While you may be interested to hear about this from a personal perspective, it's important to note that it affects more than just children. Consider the 1976 work of James Pennebaker and Deborah Yates Sanders from the University of Texas.

They placed signs in men's toilets asking them not to graffiti. Sometimes the signs were polite and said, "Please do not write on the walls." On other occasions they were stern and said, "Do NOT write on the walls!" The researchers then rotated the signs every two hours. At the end of each stint they counted the amount of graffiti on the sign.

They discovered that the authoritarian style provoked significantly more reactance: there was nearly twice as much graffiti compared to when the polite message was used.

Pennebaker's research suggests that you need to temper your language when trying to change the behaviour of others. It's often better to charm rather than cajole.

> You need to temper your language when trying to change the behaviour of others. It's often better to charm rather than cajole.

Let's look at how you can turn people's desire for freedom of choice to your advantage.

How can you apply this bias?

Knowing that it's sometimes better to lay on the charm is only so useful. What we really need to know is in which situations we should be most wary of reactance. Psychologists have identified three moments relevant to marketers.

1. Be wary of triggering reactance when there is a power imbalance with the audience

The first area concerns the authority of the communicator. Pennebaker's bathroom study tested this. Sometimes he attributed the command forbidding graffiti to the chief of police, a high-authority figure; sometimes to the university groundsperson, a low-authority figure.

Changing the status of the communicator significantly influenced the reactions of passers-by. There was twice as much graffiti when the dictate came from chief of police rather than the groundsperson.

So, be particularly wary about triggering reactance if there is a power imbalance between your brand and the recipient of your communications. Say, for example, it's a message coming from HMRC mandating the prompt return of a benefits form. In that scenario, counter-intuitively it might be best to soften the language or consider delivering the message via a third party.

2. Avoid overly assertive messages when communicating with your loyal customers

The second nuance concerns the consumer-brand relationship. In 2017 Gavan Fitzsimons from Duke University asked 162 participants to name a clothing brand. Sometimes he asked people to choose a brand that they had used for a long time and felt a degree of loyalty towards. On other occasions he asked the participants to think of a brand they had used only briefly and felt minimal loyalty to. He defined the first group as having a committed relationship and the second group an uncommitted relationship with the brand in question.

He then showed the participants one of two ads with their brand's name embedded in it. Some saw what Fitzsimons termed a non-assertive ad which had the message "Winter Collection 2012". Others saw an assertive ad which had an additional demand: "Buy Now!"

Finally, he asked participants to indicate whether the ad was likeable or not likeable. Fitzsimons found that committed shoppers liked the assertive ad 20% less than the non-assertive ad. In contrast, there were no significant differences in preference among uncommitted consumers.

The psychologist argued that, "This occurs because committed brand relationships have stronger compliance norms than uncommitted brands." In other words, the deeper a relationship, the more an assertive message feels like it impinges on our freedom. That increased pressure to comply increases the likelihood of reactance.

So, you might get away with a hard sell among new customers, but this behaviour is more likely to backfire among your most enthusiastic buyers. Tailor your communications accordingly.

3. Take culture into account

The final nuance is a cultural one. In 2009, Eva Jonas from the University of Salzburg investigated cross-cultural differences in reactance. She found that people from a more individualistic culture reported 22% more reactance when their own freedom was threatened than people from a more collectivistic society. That means if you're running a campaign in the United States or the UK you should be warier of reactance than if you were targeting people in China or South Korea.[1]

---

1   Geert Hofstede, from Maastricht University in the Netherlands, has categorised most countries on a continuum from collectivistic to individualistic. You can view the cultural orientation of countries here: www.hofstede-insights.com/product/compare-countries.

You are free to ignore the next section of this chapter

So far we have discussed *when* you should be wary of reactance but the next question is *how* you can minimise the risk of reactance. I'll cover three suggestions.

4. Harness the 'but you are free' principle

Let's begin with a 2000 study conducted by Nicolas Guéguen from South-Brittany University and Alexandre Pascual from the University of Bordeaux.

Guéguen approached 80 strangers and asked them for money to take a bus. He made the request in one of two ways. Sometimes he said "Sorry, would you have some coins to take the bus, please?"; on other occasions he modified the request and said "Sorry, would you have some coins to take the bus, please? *But you are free to accept or to refuse.*"

When participants were bluntly asked to give money, the compliance rate was 10%. However, when the experimenter highlighted the participant's right to decline, the compliance rate jumped to 48%.

Think about the scale of that change for a while: that's nearly a five-fold increase in donation rates. Many behavioural science studies eke out a 10% or 15% improvement. This is a highly effective intervention.

Additionally, the effect extended beyond the proportion of people who donated. The level of donations was also boosted. The 'but you are free' subjects gave on average $1.04, more than double the 48c given by those in the control condition. Simply by drawing attention to the fact that people had the right to refuse (something

THE ILLUSION OF CHOICE

which of course existed anyway), Guéguen created a step-change in compliance.

This experiment isn't a one-off. In 2013, Christopher Carpenter from Western Illinois University conducted a meta-analysis of 42 studies relating to this tactic and found that it increased compliance across a variety of settings. So, whether you are making charitable or commercial requests you should consider applying this principle. After making a demand which might provoke reactance, add in the key phrase: 'but you are free to accept or to refuse.' Reminding people of their freedom to say no avoids reactance.

5. Involve people in the decision

An alternative angle is to provide people with a degree of control. Crucially, this control doesn't have to be meaningful. Even a cosmetic element of input can help.

The evidence for this comes from a 2014 study by Cait Lamberton from the University of Pittsburgh, Jan-Emmanuel De Neve from UCL and Michael Norton from Harvard University. They asked 182 students to rate their enjoyment of 12 pictures on a nine-point scale.

The psychologists told the participants that they would be paid $10 for their time but that they would have to return $3 of their reward as a lab tax. They were instructed to put the fee in an envelope and hand it to the experimenter once they had finished their task.

The convoluted method of collecting the tax was designed to allow the participants to easily cheat and keep some of the cash. Quite a few did! In fact, 45% left the envelope empty and 3% left only a partial amount.

However, the psychologists repeated the experiment with a slight twist. A second group of participants was told that they could advise the lab manager on how the tax was to be used. For example, they could suggest the funds were used to buy drinks and snacks for future participants. Even though the group's suggestions were merely advisory there was a sizable impact on compliance: 68% left the full amount of money in the envelope. That's an increase of 30% on the control.

Giving people a voice increased their willingness to comply.

6. Remove the possibility of change

Our final tactic for avoiding reactance is focussed on you, the marketer. If you have to mandate a change in behaviour, make sure you're certain of your approach.

This point is supported by work from Kristin Laurin and Aaron Kay from the University of Waterloo and Gavan Fitzsimons from Duke University.

In 2012 they told participants that experts had concluded that lower speed limits in cities improved safety. However, the psychologists split the participants into three groups and told each of them a slightly different story.

The first group, the control, were given no additional information. The second group were told that their government had definitely decided to reduce speed limits. Finally, a third group were told that legislation would come into effect if a majority of officials voted in support, which they likely would. Crucially, in this scenario they left the possibility that the legislation might be overturned.

Participants were then questioned about how much they supported the legislation and how much they would be annoyed by it. Laurin found that participants who were told that the legislation was definitely occurring were much more positive towards it than the group in the ambiguous scenario. It seems that the certainty allowed them to begin rationalising the legislation change.

In this chapter, we've discussed how people desire to feel in control. In the next chapter we'll discuss a slightly different angle:

how those who assert their freedom by breaking conventions tend to benefit...

REFERENCES

'American Graffiti: Effects of Authority and Reactance Arousal' by James Pennebaker and Deborah Yates Sanders [*Personality and Social Psychology Bulletin*, Vol. 2, No. 3, pp. 264–267, 1976]

'Just do it! Why committed consumers react negatively to assertive ads' by Yael Zemack-Rugar, Sarah Moore and Gavan Fitzsimons [*Journal of Consumer Psychology*, Vol. 27, No. 3, pp. 287–301, 2017]

'Culture, Self and the Emergence of Reactance: Is there a "Universal" Freedom?' by Eva Jonas, Verena Graupmann, Daniela Niesta Kayser, Mark Zanna, Eva Traut-Mattausch and Dieter Frey [*Journal of Experimental Social Psychology*, Vol. 45, No. 5, pp. 1068–1080, 2009]

'Evocation of freedom and compliance: The "but you are free of..." technique' by Nicolas Guéguen and Alexandre Pascual [*Current Research in Social Psychology*, Vol. 5, pp. 264–270, 2000]

'A Meta-Analysis of the Effectiveness of the "But You Are Free" Compliance Gaining Techniques' by Christopher Carpenter [*Communication Studies*, Vol. 64, No. 1, pp. 6–17, 2013]

'Eliciting Taxpayer Preferences Increases Tax Compliance' by Cait Lamberton, Jan-Emmanuel De Neve and Michael Norton [*SSRN*, 2014]

'Reactance versus rationalization: divergent responses to policies that constrain freedom' by Kristin Laurin, Aaron Kay and Gavan Fitzsimons [*Psychological Science*, Vol. 23, No. 2, pp. 205–209, 2012]

13

THE RED SNEAKERS EFFECT

THE BOARD MEETING has dragged on for an hour. Most of the seemingly interminable meeting has been taken up with a tetchy debate on the company's policy towards working from home. Wil, the managing director, has been calling for flexibility while John, the COO, has vociferously argued the case for everyone returning full-time.

Both proposals have their merits but, on balance, you side with the managing director.

The chairperson draws the debate to a close and puts the matter to the vote. She goes round the table and asks people which option they prefer. One by one your colleagues voice their support for the chief operating officer.

It's your turn soon. You begin to wonder whether maybe your colleagues might be right? Perhaps it really is best for morale if everyone returns to the office full-time.

THE ILLUSION OF CHOICE

Y ou're not alone in feeling pressure to conform. It's a tendency demonstrated in one of the most famous experiments in the history of psychology, conducted by Solomon Asch just after the end of World War II.

When Asch was a teacher at Swarthmore College, he asked participants to take part in a supposed vision test. The subjects were shown a piece of card with a line on it. They then had to select which line from a range of three others was the same length.

It was an easy task. In Asch's words, a "clear and simple issue of fact". So simple in fact, that when people did it alone, they answered correctly more than 99% of the time.

However, in the main experiment Asch's participants didn't complete the task alone, but in a group of seven or nine. The participant thought these were just subjects like themselves, whereas in reality they were confederates of Asch who had been instructed how to answer. Each participant took part in 18 trials in total and the confederates gave the same wrong answer on 12 of the trials.

Asch was interested in how the real participant would react. Would they change their response to fit in with the group?

The results showed a remarkable degree of conformity. Three-quarters of the participants conformed at least once by giving the wrong answer. Overall, one-third of the answers were incorrect.

Let's look at the advantages you can find in the tendency of many people to conform.

How can you apply this bias?

1. Breaking conventions signals status

This tendency to mimic behaviour has been demonstrated in many studies. It seems to stem from a desire for acceptance and to avoid the possibility of negative sanctions.

This suggests brands might benefit from communicating that they are the choice of the majority. This is true in many circumstances and something I covered at length in *The Choice Factory*.

However, there are some occasions when flouting group norms is beneficial for a communicator. This stems from the fact that there is a risk that breaking these norms might generate social disapproval. If that is the case, the people most able to deviate from conventions are those who have high status. They're the people who have enough reputational capital to bear these costs.

This topic has been explored by Francesca Gino from the Harvard Business School. In 2011 she conducted a field study at the Association for Consumer Research conference. Like other academic conferences, this one had a convention whereby people were expected to dress smartly.

Gino recorded how formally individual attendees were dressed and, in order to gauge the status of the academic, the number of peer-reviewed papers they had published.

Gino found an inverse correlation between smartness of dress and the volume of papers they had published – the most successful academics were indeed the ones most likely to break conventions.

But while this study demonstrates that those with high status are more likely to break conventions, it doesn't reveal how others interpret that behaviour. That gap led Silvia Bellezza, Francesca Gino and Anat Keinan to run a follow-up study. They asked 159 respondents to rate the status and competence of a professor, based on a short description of them.

Participants were told about a professor who either conformed ("Mike typically wears a tie to work and is clean-shaven") or did not conform ("Mike typically wears a t-shirt to work and has a beard").

They were then asked to rate the competence of the professor and how well respected they were on a seven-point scale. Respondents rated the nonconforming professor at 5.35 compared to just 5.00 for the conforming academic. That's a statistically significant 14% swing.

In Gino's words:

> Since nonconformity often has a social cost, observers may infer that a nonconforming individual is in a powerful position that allows her to risk the social costs of nonconformity without fear of losing her place in the social hierarchy.

Gino termed this idea the red sneakers effect. This name came from the fact that at the time of her research many high-profile tech entrepreneurs were flouting business dress codes. Rather than attend important meetings in a suit and tie, they chose sweatshirts and trainers (or sneakers) – sometimes red ones.

2. The advertising application

But how relevant are these studies? Gino's experiments are fascinating but the situations she described – concerning dress codes and shaving – are a long way from ads. Can we extrapolate the findings to brands?

With that conundrum in mind, in 2020 Duncan Willett, Sumran Kaul and I tested the impact of the 'red sneakers effect' in a more commercial setting. We showed a group of participants four obscure bottles of craft beer with eye-catching designs. Three of the labels were designed in broadly the same style, whereas the final beer had a markedly different style. Participants then had to rate the quality of the beer.

While this was happening, another large group of participants were shown four beer bottles. We included two of the beers from the first experiment – the uniquely styled bottle and one of the others. The remaining two beers were both in the same style as the previously uniquely styled label.

This experimental design allowed us to compare the ratings of the same bottle design in a scenario when it was either conforming to, or breaking, conventions.

Just as the red sneakers effect suggests, the bottle design was rated higher when it broke the surrounding conventions. It was a smaller effect than Gino found – a 5% improvement – but the convention broken was a minor one; just the surrounding bottles, rather than a wide-scale societal one. It might well be that bigger conventions draw bigger improvements.

3. Beware the nuances of the red sneakers effect

Before you rush off to break your category conventions, it's worth reflecting on some of the nuances of the bias. The red sneakers effect only has a positive impact if a few qualifying criteria are met.

First, the brand in question needs to already have a degree of status. This was shown in the experiment with the unshaven professor. Sometimes, the psychologists said the professor was at a prestigious university, sometimes a non-prestigious one.

The benefits of nonconformity only held true for professors working at the prestigious institution. The nonconformist professor at the low-ranking university was rated as 8% less competent than the conformist at the same institution.

Nonconforming behaviours boost perceived competence and status – but only if the person in question is already regarded as having high status. The bias accentuates, rather than mitigates, existing status.

You need to honestly ask yourself whether your brand has the necessary stature to harness the red sneakers effect. That is easier said than done. People tend to overestimate their abilities.[2] Marketers are no exception.

Along with the agency The Marketing Practice, I ran a survey among 213 marketers. The results were clear cut: 84% of the participants thought they were better at their job than their peers, and 45% rated themselves 'much better'.

This overconfidence extended to the company they worked for: 79% of respondents thought their company was better than their competitors. Additionally, when we told them to imagine a scenario where they were pitching against two competitors for a new piece of business, 75% of them thought they had a better chance of success than the odds alone would suggest.

So, if you think your brand doesn't have the status to apply the red sneakers effect, you're probably right. If you think you do, then it's probably worth getting a second opinion!

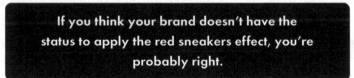

If you think your brand doesn't have the status to apply the red sneakers effect, you're probably right.

4. The need to show intention

The second consideration is that you need to ensure any norm-breaking is seen as deliberate.

---

2   My favourite example of our overconfidence in our abilities comes from a study by Constantine Sedikides from Southampton University. In 2014 he ran a study among offenders at a prison in South East England. Even this group of miscreants rated themselves as more moral, kinder to others, more self-controlled, more trustworthy and more honest than an average member of the community.

That insight comes from a study where Gino asked 141 participants to read a vignette about a man, Charles, who attended a formal black-tie party for his golf club.

He was described as either wearing a black bow tie (conforming dress style) or a red bow tie (nonconforming dress style). Further to this, participants were also told whether Charles broke the convention deliberately or by mistake.

Participants then guessed Charles's status as a member of the golf club and performance as a player. When the nonconforming behaviour was deliberate, Charles's status increased by 17% (vs the black tie), whereas when the deviation from norms was a mistake, his status reduced by 5%.

If you're going to harness the red sneakers effect, make sure you do it with confidence. Your audience needs to know it was a deliberate act. One way to do that is through premium pricing. In the words of the academics:

Price might be a valuable driver of perceived intentionality in marketing nonconforming products. Nonconforming brands that are associated with premium prices signal that the nonconforming individual can afford conventional status symbols.

5. The need for audience familiarity

The third condition that mediates the impact of the red sneakers effect is the familiarity of the audience with the norm being broken.

This insight comes from a study completed by the same psychologists in Milan. They enlisted 109 women, 52 of whom worked in luxury boutiques like Armani or Burberry. The remainder were members of the public recruited at a nearby railway station.

Participants were asked to read a vignette describing a shopper. Some heard about a character that abided by dress conventions:

THE ILLUSION OF CHOICE

Imagine a woman is entering a luxury boutique in downtown Milan during winter. She looks approximately 35 years old. She is wearing a dress and fur coat.

Others heard about a nonconformist who dressed surprisingly casually, in gym clothes and a jacket.

Shop assistants, who were familiar with the environment, rated the status of the nonconformist shopper higher. On a seven-point scale they rated the nonconformist at 4.9, compared to 3.8 for the conformist. That's a 29% higher status rating for the nonconforming shopper. In contrast, members of the public, who were typically unfamiliar with the context, rated the shopper who abided by the dress norms as higher status than the nonconformist (a 5.7 rating compared to 3.5).

This study suggests that the value of the red sneakers effect is greatest for those most familiar with your brand or the category.

The red sneakers effect is one of my favourite biases, but that doesn't mean you should use it on every campaign. As Gino has demonstrated, it only works in certain circumstances – for example, if you have a degree of status.

However, if you harness the red sneakers effect in the right circumstances, then your brand is likely to be seen as higher status. Interestingly, that uplift will tend to spill over into areas beyond perceived status. That occurrence is known as the halo effect and it's the subject of our next chapter...

'Effects of group pressure upon the modification and distortion of judgments' by Solomon Asch, in H. Guetzkow (Eds.), *Groups, leadership and men; research in human relations* (pp. 177–190, 1951)

'The Red Sneakers Effect: Inferring Status and Competence from Signals of Nonconformity' by Silvia Bellezza, Francesca Gino and Anat Keinan [*Journal of Consumer Research*, Vol. 41, No. 1, pp. 35–54, 2014]

Behavioural Science: What does it mean for B2B marketers by The Marketing Practice and Richard Shotton [2018] retrieved from: https://25865525. fs1.hubspotusercontent-eu1.net/hubfs/25865525/Blogs/Reports/ Behavioural-Science-for-B2B-marketers-TMP-research.pdf

'Behind bars but above the bar: Prisoners consider themselves more prosocial than non-prisoners' by Constantine Sedikides, Rosie Meek, Mark Alicke and Sarah Taylor [*British Journal of Social Psychology*, Vol. 53, No. 2, pp. 396–403, 2013]

14

THE HALO EFFECT

TWICE THIS WEEK you'd caught yourself squinting at blurry writing on far-off signs, so you booked an eye test for this afternoon. Frustratingly, the branch you normally use had no availability, so you made do with an alternative chain.

When you arrive for the test, there's a short queue at reception. After a few minutes, the optometrist bounds towards you with their hand thrust out. Their handshake is limp and clammy. Unkind thoughts race through your mind. Was trying this new place a mistake after all? Are they going to be as thorough as normal?

YOU'RE NOT ALONE in drawing conclusions about a person's entire character from a single trait. In 1920 Edward Thorndike, a psychologist at Columbia University, showed that making judgements in this way is typical. He asked army officers to rate a new intake of soldiers on 31 attributes, covering areas from physique to initiative, loyalty to neatness.

Thorndike found that the ratings correlated remarkably strongly, even across unrelated attributes. For example, superiors who scored a soldier highly on one metric, such as appearance, would rate the same soldier as above average in other areas, such as leadership. Thorndike termed the tendency for the ratings of one positive trait to influence the others, the 'halo effect'.[1]

Experimental evidence

The evidence extends beyond these suspicious correlations. In 1977 Richard Nisbett from the University of Michigan and Timothy Wilson from the University of Virginia tested the halo effect in a more controlled manner.

They asked 118 students to watch a video of a Belgian lecturer who spoke English with a pronounced accent. The students were split into two groups. Half of the students watched a video showing the instructor behaving in a warm and friendly way. The remainder saw the same person acting in a cold and impersonal way. His mannerisms and accent were unchanged in both settings.

The participants then rated the lecturer in terms of likeability, appearance, mannerisms and his accent. As you might expect, the warm instructor was rated as 72% more likeable than the cold instructor.

However, he was also rated higher in terms of his appearance (around +100%), accent (around +100%) and mannerisms (around +53%). That's more interesting – after all, *objectively* a person's likeability shouldn't affect ratings of their looks or accent.

---

1   The halo effect is generally used to describe how one positive trait influences people's evaluation of other unrelated traits. There is a related insight called the horns effect which refers to the same situation but with negative characteristics, although of course in this scenario other unrelated characteristics are judged worse. The initial study into this comes from 1974 and the work of Harold Sigove and David Landy.

But just as Thorndike would have predicted, that's not what happened.

The halo effect doesn't just affect soldiers and students. It occurs in commercial settings too. Joanna Stanley and I told 404 Brits about a fictional greengrocer and asked the participants to speculate on how broad a range of products the store stocked. The twist in the experiment was that half the participants were told the store had a typo on their sign – a rogue apostrophe. Half heard about no such grammatical crime.

The results were clear. The group who heard about the typo were 17% more likely to assume that the store had a poor range than the group who didn't hear about the error.

From an objective perspective, a greengrocer's grammatical ability is distinct from the breadth of the store's range. However, that's not how people reacted in practice. Respondents used a tangible factor that's easy to spot (the slapdash sign) to make predictions about unrelated, but harder to ascertain, factors (the product range).

> Consumers use tangible factors that are easy to spot to make predictions about unrelated, but harder to ascertain, factors.

Why does the halo effect occur?

We shouldn't be surprised that the halo effect crops up so regularly. After all, it serves a valuable purpose. It makes life manageable.

Evaluating every brand we encounter on multiple criteria would be complex and time-consuming. It's quicker to use the most salient characteristic of a brand as a proxy for other more intangible ones.

As Daniel Kahneman says, "This is the essence of intuitive heuristics: when faced with a difficult question, we often answer an easier one instead, usually without noticing the substitution."

How can you apply this bias?

1. You can achieve your goals obliquely as well as directly

The halo effect suggests brands can achieve their objectives obliquely. Since a stand-out success in one area influences people's perception of unrelated attributes, it means that target metrics can be addressed indirectly. You can impact your target metric, say quality perceptions, by boosting another metric, say likeability.

But just because you *can* do something, it doesn't necessarily mean that you *should*. After all, while the halo effect reveals that many metrics correlate, it doesn't show they move in lockstep. And if metrics aren't perfectly correlated, it means an oblique approach might be inefficient. Continuing the example from above, you could move the likeability metric significantly, but achieve a measly shift in quality perceptions.

So, the question becomes: when is using this tactic worthwhile? When does it make sense to adopt this oblique approach?

2. Focus on the halo effect if your brand is little known

Barbara Koltuv at Columbia University has identified one effective application of the halo effect. She has shown that when the brand is relatively unknown the halo effect is particularly powerful.

In 1962 she read people a series of short character descriptions, such as: "A young man who you know and like" or "An old man whom you dislike and don't know well".

The participants were then asked to think of an acquaintance matching that description. Finally, the subjects evaluated the genuine acquaintance on 47 personality traits, such as whether they were easy-going or hostile, loyal or jealous.

When participants described a person they were unfamiliar with, there was a greater degree of correlation between their traits than when they were discussing a familiar person. In other words, the halo effect was more powerful.

This suggests the halo effect is particularly prevalent in situations of uncertainty. If we've had minimal dealings with a person or brand, we've had fewer chances to make independent inferences about all of their characteristics. So, the halo effect is most powerful when you're launching a brand or working on a brand with limited awareness.

3. Prioritise the halo effect if you need to convey intangible attributes

The second, and more important, situation where the halo effect is significant is when boosting an intangible metric. Imagine, for example, a brand is promoting a toothpaste by making claims about its plaque-fighting ability. In that situation, it's hard for a consumer to evaluate the believability of those claims. How does the shopper know if the brand is exaggerating the benefits or telling the truth? That difficulty means the consumer is disproportionately influenced by other, less ambiguous, data points.

That's not speculation. In 1978, William James from the University of Alabama investigated the effect of ambiguity on the strength of the halo effect. He asked participants to rate 17 cities on nine attributes. Some attributes were unambiguous, such as the population or the annual amount of snowfall, whereas others were ambiguous, such as the pleasantness of the summer or the quality of the cultural activities.

James then measured the degree to which the attributes correlated. He found that the ambiguous factors correlated far more than the unambiguous ones (0.34 vs 0.15).

In the words of Phil Rosenzweig, professor at IMD and author of the book, *The Halo Effect*:

> We tend to grasp information that is relevant, tangible, and appears to be objective, and then make attributions about other features that are more vague or ambiguous.

So, ask yourself, are you trying to shift brand characteristics that are vague and ambiguous? If so, an oblique approach is best.

However, that recommendation just raises another question, namely *what* tangible metrics should you focus on instead. Knowing *when* to draw on the halo effect is important, but we also need to understand *how* to harness it: what facet of a brand's personality should you boost if you are avoiding directly addressing your target objective?

Well, we know that the tangibility of an attribute is key. It has to be a characteristic that an audience can easily grasp.

There are two characteristics that people find easy to make snap judgements about: likeability and attractiveness. For both, there is proof that they can stimulate the halo effect.

4. Tap into the halo effect by emphasising your brand's attractiveness

Let's start with attractiveness. There's a longstanding idea that beauty is indicative of other attributes. As far back as 1820, John

CHAPTER 14: THE HALO EFFECT

Keats famously ended his poem, *Ode on a Grecian Urn*, with the lines:

Beauty is truth, truth beauty,—that is all
Ye know on earth, and all ye need to know.

Keats was ahead of his time. Modern experiments have demonstrated that attractiveness is a tangible characteristic about which people make snap judgements. It's also a characteristic that has been shown to harness the halo effect.

In 1972, Karen Dion from the University of Minnesota asked 60 participants to look at pictures of three faces and judge their personalities and life success. She asked questions such as, did the people appear interesting? Did they look genuine? How happy were they?

Dion had selected the photos carefully. A previous study had rated the looks of the subjects – one was deemed attractive, one average and the other unattractive.

The attractiveness of the subjects in the photo affected how their characters were evaluated. Overall, attractive individuals were judged to have 16% more favourable personality traits, as well as enjoying greater life success compared to unattractive individuals.

The halo effect from attractiveness seems to have real-world implications. In 1974, Michael Efran and E. W. J. Patterson from the University of Toronto studied the results of the Canadian federal elections. They found that good-looking candidates received more than two and a half times as many votes as ugly ones.

Of course, you might be thinking that a politician's looks are a long way from your marketing concerns. But the principle – that people infer strength in other attributes from looks – has been shown to apply closer to home.

In 1995, researchers Masaaki Kurosu and Kaori Kashimura from the Hitachi Design Centre asked 252 participants to test 26 layouts of an ATM's user interface. Participants were asked to rate each interface in three areas: appearance, how easy they predicted it will be to use, and later, actual usability.

The researchers found that the more attractive the interface, the more likely participants were to expect ease-of-use. However, appearance was not correlated with actual usability. These results show that perceived usability is strongly affected by aesthetic aspects.

These findings should interest marketers. If you want to boost intangible value, like quality, then boosting design attractiveness is one way to achieve that. In many ways this is a more manageable task for a marketer, as you can actually make a beautiful product, whereas for intangible values like trust you can only make claims.

5. Harness the halo effect by boosting your likeability

Next, let's consider likeability. Just as with beauty, people tend to assume likeable people and products embody other positive attributes.

In 2001 Carolyn Nicholson from Stetson University, Florida, and Larry Compeau and Rajesh Sethi from Clarkson University, New York, explored the relationship between likeability and trustworthiness between a sales rep and a buyer.

They asked 238 business owners and general managers to rate their major supplier's sales rep's likeability and trustworthiness. The results showed that likeability was a major influence on their trustworthiness; the higher the score, the more trustworthy they viewed the rep.

Once again, the evidence extends beyond correlations. Joanna Stanley and I recruited 161 participants and told them a story about

CHAPTER 14: THE HALO EFFECT

visiting a restaurant. At the end, we asked the participants how likely it was that the owner paid his tax on time.

The twist in the experiment was that half were told the owner had welcomed them in a friendly manner, half that he had behaved sullenly. Even though bonhomie isn't genuinely correlated with financial probity, it influenced the participants' perceptions. People were 37% more likely to think the owner would pay his tax on time when he behaved in a friendly way, compared to when he exhibited more stand-offish behaviour.

Just as Rosenzweig predicts, evaluating an intangible quality is tricky, so without even noticing it people use a substitute, simpler question, such as 'Is this person likeable?' and rely on the associated answer.

This is a practically applicable finding. On many occasions brands need to improve the perception of their intangible attributes, like trust or quality. Too often marketers mistakenly tackle this head on. The experiments you've just read about suggest proceeding obliquely and bolstering likeability.

Luckily, that's an easier metric to shift. In a 30-second ad a brand can make the audience laugh, be witty and generally likeable. It can *demonstrate* these characteristics. However, when it comes to trust or quality in an ad, you can only *claim* these characteristics. That's much less believable.

However, all this discussion of likeability might be triggering a few awkward thoughts in your mind. It's easy to talk about likeability, but how do you demonstrate it? That's the real challenge. Well, that's the topic for the next chapter.

REFERENCES

'A constant error in psychological ratings' by Edward Thorndike [*Journal of Applied Psychology*, Vol. 4, No. 1, pp. 25–29, 1920]

THE ILLUSION OF CHOICE

'The halo effect: Evidence for unconscious alteration of judgments' by Richard Nisbett and Timothy Wilson [*Journal of Personality and Social Psychology*, Vol. 35, No. 4, pp. 250–256, 1977]

'Some characteristics of intrajudge trait intercorrelations' by Barbara Koltuv [*Psychological Monographs: General and Applied*, Vol. 76, No. 33, pp. 1–33, 1962]

'Halo Effects and Location Preferences' by William James and Forest Carter [*Advances in Consumer Research*, Vol. 5, No. 1, pp. 474–476, 1978]

The Halo Effect, by Phil Rosenweig [2007]

'The role of interpersonal liking in building trust in long-term channel relationships' by Carolyn Nicholson, Larry Compeau and Rajesh Sethi [*Journal of the Academy of Marketing Science*, Vol. 29, No. 3, pp. 3–15, 2001]

'Voters vote beautiful: The effect of physical appearance on a national election' by Michael Efran and E. W. J. Patterson [*Canadian Journal of Behavioural Science*, Vol. 6, No. 4, pp.352–356, 1976]

'What is beautiful is good' by Karen Dion, Ellen Berscheid and Elaine Walster [*Journal of Personality and Social Psychology*, Vol. 24, No. 3, pp. 285–290, 1972]

'Beauty is talent: Task evaluation as a function of the performer's physical attractiveness' by Harold Sigove and David Landy [*Journal of Personality and Social Psychology*, Vol. 29, No. 3, pp. 299–304, 1974]

15

THE WISDOM
OF WIT

YOUR ENERGY LEVELS are sagging so you head out of the office for a caffeine hit. A quick espresso to perk you up.

After finishing off the dregs you catch the eye of the waiter and, by mimicking your signature in the air, request the bill.

While waiting to pay, you mull over how generous the tip should be. You don't have a great selection of change so you've the option of leaving roughly 10% or 20%.

You think back to the service. The waiter was cheerful, even managing to crack a joke or two.

You plump for 20%, no point being stingy.

YOUR REACTION TO the waiter's light-heartedness isn't a one-off. Research by Nicolas Guéguen suggests that serving staff who attempt the odd joke tend to be rewarded with larger tips.

In 2002 Guéguen ran an experiment among 211 customers at a

seaside bar. When these drinkers had finished their espressos the waiter brought the bill, which either came on its own or with a joke attached to it. The gag went as follows:

An Eskimo had been waiting for his girlfriend in front of a movie theatre for a long time, and it was getting colder and colder. After a while, shivering with cold and rather infuriated, he opened his coat and drew out a thermometer. He then said loudly, "If she is not here at 15, I'm going!"

Among the control group – those who didn't receive a joke – 19% left a tip. In contrast, 42% of customers receiving the joke left a tip. The attempt at humour also affected the size of the tips – customers who received the joke gave a tip of 23%, significantly more than the 16% left by those who just received the bill.

It's an interesting study as it suggests that humour can boost revenues in a commercial setting.

But that might sound like a statement of the obvious; don't advertisers already know that?

Well, perhaps once, but it seems that as an industry, we're growing more earnest as the years go by.

The trend started over 15 years ago, according to Kantar's analysis of over 200,000 ads from around the globe. In 2004, 53% of ads, just over half, were funny or light-hearted – or at least tried to be. But this proportion has been steadily shrinking, and now ads are more serious than ever, with just 34% making any attempt at humour.

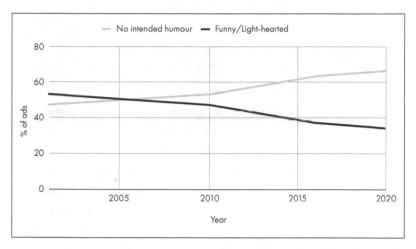

Source: adapted from Kantar's analysis.

The reason for this decline isn't clear.

It could be that more campaigns run in multiple countries and there's a fear that some jokes don't travel well. Another plausible explanation is that the growth of sombre ads pontificating on a brand's purpose leaves fewer opportunities for laughs. There's even an argument that awards juries, composed of a mix of international luminaries, favour the visual over the verbal. Since agencies use their performance at award shows to drum up new business, this has led to a decline in the appeal of humour from a selfish perspective.

But whatever the explanation, avoiding humour might be a mistake. There are a couple of reasons why.

First, funny is memorable.

In 2014 Gurinder Bains and colleagues at Loma Linda University, California, carried out a study among 20 older people. All participants took a test to establish baseline memory. This involved recalling lists of words. Half of the participants then watched a 20-minute humorous video, while the remaining half – the control group – sat quietly for 20 minutes. The psychologists then repeated the recall test. Both groups improved upon their baseline scores, but the memory boost among the comedy group was more than double that achieved by the control group – 44% vs 20%.

But humour doesn't just boost memorability in lab settings. There's evidence it works in the real world too.

Avner Ziv, a psychologist at Tel Aviv University, carried out research among students taking a statistics course. For the study, published in the *Journal of Experimental Education* in 2014, students were split into two groups. One group was taught the course material with humour, the other heard it straight. And the results were clear – the class who laughed scored 11% higher in their statistics exam.

It doesn't take a huge leap of imagination to see how these findings apply to advertising. The primary goal of any advertiser is memorability: without bringing your brand to mind, your customer can't even consider a purchase.

> **The primary goal of any advertiser is memorability.**

But there's another reason why it pays to make them laugh: there's a strong connection between wit and status. In a 2017 study by T. Bradford Bitterly, Alison Wood Brooks and Maurice E. Schweitzer, participants were asked to write and present testimonials for a fictional travel company, VisitSwitzerland. The group didn't know that the first two participants to present were in fact researchers. One gave a straight testimonial, discussing the mountains and how great they are for skiing and hiking. The other added humour: "The mountains are great for skiing and hiking and the flag is a big plus!"

When the participants rated the presenters, those who introduced a bit of levity were seen as 5% more competent and 11% more confident, and were rated as having 37% higher status.

But the proof stretches beyond one-off studies. While individual experiments are useful, the most robust evidence comes from a meta-analysis. Here a researcher combs through all the existing high-quality research and, using a variety of statistical techniques, combines the results to find common patterns.

The latest meta-analysis on the role of humour in advertising was conducted in 2009 by Martin Eisend, a professor of marketing at the European University Viadrina in Frankfurt. He managed to find 38 high-quality papers on the topic published between 1960 and 2004.

Eisend found seven statistically significant findings. Humorous ads had a significant beneficial correlation with:

- attitudes towards the ad
- attitudes towards the brand
- attention
- positive emotions
- a reduction in negative emotions
- and most importantly, purchase intent.

However, there was one negative correlation – with credibility.

The most sizeable effects were the link between humorous ads and improved attention and attitudes towards the ad.

It's not just academics that have spotted the benefits of humour. Les Binet and Peter Field have analysed 243 case studies entered for the IPA Effectiveness Awards between 2012 and 2020. They found that the campaigns that contained an element of humour generated 1.7 very large business effects, compared to just 1.4 for the non-humorous ads.

How can you apply this bias?

1. Give more consideration to humour as a tactic

The weight of evidence suggests that marketers are wrong to shift away from humour. In general, if you want to grab people's attention, engender a positive set of associations or increase their purchase intent, there is strong evidence that communicating in a humorous way is an effective tactic.

Brands would do well to heed the words of Martin Boase, founder of the legendary ad agency BMP:

> We believe that if you are going to invite yourself into someone's living room you have a duty not to shout at them or bore them or insult their intelligence. On the other hand, if you are a charming guest and you entertain them or amuse them or tell them something interesting, then they might like you a little bit better and they may be more inclined to buy your brand.

2. Turn to humour when you're communicating uncomfortable matters

However, rather than just asking *whether* humour is effective we should also ask *when* it is effective.

One situation in which humour is particularly effective is if you're communicating a topic that makes people uncomfortable. For example, a gym advertising to couch potatoes about the danger of a sedentary lifestyle. In situations like this your plans risk being derailed by the 'ostrich effect'; the finding that people tend to avoid negative information.

The most relevant evidence for this bias comes from a 2009 study conducted by George Loewenstein and Duane Seppi from Carnegie Mellon University. They studied how often stock market investors in the US and Sweden checked their portfolios using log-in data from the Swedish Premium Pension Authority and the investment manager, Vanguard.

The psychologists found a different pattern of behaviour depending on whether the stock market was rising or falling. When the market rose by 1% there was a 5–6% increase in the US investors checking their portfolios and a 1% increase among the Swedes. In the words of the psychologists, people "avoid exposing [themselves] to information that [they] fear will cause psychological discomfort."

Humour has a potential role here. If people bury their heads in the sand when confronted with undesirable information, can humour neutralise some of that negativity?

The 2012 public safety message *Dumb Ways to Die* from Melbourne Metro suggests so. The Metro wanted to reduce the number of rail accidents involving young people but recognised that describing the dangers in graphic detail would frighten people, and they might not engage deeply.

Instead they drew their audience towards the message by creating a morbidly funny jingle describing a macabre list of ways to die – with being hit by a train as "the dumbest way to die".

If you haven't heard the song, the opening lines give a flavour of the dark humour:

Set fire to your hair
Poke a stick at a grizzly bear
Eat medicine that's out of date
Use your private parts as piranha bait
Dumb ways to die
So many dumb ways to die

The video of the song has been watched 200 million times and it is the most shared public service message of all time, with five million people passing it on to their friends. Most importantly, it changed behaviour. There was a 21% reduction in accidents in the three months after the ad aired compared to the same time period the year before.

Sarah Carter, one of the ad industry's most respected planners, puts it brilliantly:

> As anyone who has successfully coaxed a toddler to eat their food by pretending a spoon was an aeroplane will know: if you can disarm you can persuade. So keep it playful. People like it this way. And it works.

3. Prioritise humorous messages among your fans

It's not just unpalatable messages that can benefit from a dash of levity. Another situation in which humour works is one where you have a strong brand, or you're targeting your fans. Here the positive effects of humour are magnified.

The evidence for this approach comes from a 1990 study conducted by Amitava Chattopadhyay and Kunal Basu from McGill University, Canada. The researchers began the study by asking 80 participants to read a description of an unfamiliar pen brand: half of them read a glowing piece, half a damning one.

Next, all the participants watched a TV ad for a pen: half saw a humorous version, half sat through a non-humorous one. In all other respects, the ads were identical.

After watching the ads, the participants answered a series of questions. Finally, as the experiment was drawing to a close the participants were offered a gift as a thank you: they could pick one of four pens to take home, either the advertised pen or one of three others.

The proportion of people who picked the advertised pen in each scenario can be seen in the table below.

	Watched humorous ad	Watched non-humorous ad
Positive impression of brand	67%	40%
Negative impression of brand	20%	38%

Source: adapted from Chattopadhyay and Basu study. Percentages refer to the number of people picking the advertised pen.

Which ad was most effective depended on the participant's prior impression of the brand. If they had been led to believe the pen was high quality, the humorous ad was by far the most effective of the two approaches.

However, the situation was flipped when participants had a negative impression of the pen brand. In this setting the non-humorous ad significantly outperformed the funny one.

This study adds further nuance to the recommendations. Humour is most effective when you have a strong brand or are targeting those predisposed to your messages, but perhaps best avoided if your brand is struggling.

4. Maximising the impact of humour: mood

The final set of experiments concerns how to maximise the impact of a funny ad. One of the most interesting findings comes from a study in 1981 led by Frank Wicker from the University of Texas at Austin. He was interested in how mood affected the appreciation of jokes.

He began the experiment by asking 125 participants to rate their mood. Next, he asked them to read 37 jokes and rate their funniness, from "not at all" to "extremely". Wicker found that the better the mood of the participant, the higher they rated the jokes. So, target people when they're in a good mood.

A word of warning though comes from a 2007 Millward Brown paper, 'Should I use humour in advertising?' They argue that while humour builds enjoyment and involvement, it is most effective when aligned with core messaging. Humour that is unrelated to the key message risks dominating the ad and drowning out your brand.

So, use wit wisely – and you should see a lift in both memorability and status of your brand. But take care to stay on-message, or you could end up doing more harm than good.

Unfortunately, we're coming to the end of our behavioural science journey. But before we finish, I've got one more set of experiments I want to share with you. I think these studies are some of the most interesting in the whole book. I hope you do too. After all, it's important to end on a high…

REFERENCES

'The Effects of a Joke on Tipping When It Is Delivered at the Same Time as the Bill' by Nicolas Guéguen [*Journal of Applied Social Psychology*, Vol. 32, No. 9 pp. 1955–1963, 2002]

'The "Strategic Sparks" Behind the 2022 Kantar Creative Effectiveness Award Winners' Kantar New Zealand www.kantarnewzealand.com/the-strategic-sparks-behind-the-2022-kantar-creative-effectiveness-award-winners

'The Effect of Humor on Short-term Memory in Older Adults: A New Component for Whole-Person Wellness' by Gurinder Singh Bains, Lee Berk, Noha Daher, Everett Lohman, Ernie Schwab, Jerrold Petrofsky and Pooja Deshpande [*Loma Linda University Electronic Theses, Dissertations & Projects*, 207, 2014]

'Teaching and Learning with Humor' by Avner Ziv [*The Journal of Experimental Education*, Vol. 57, No. 1, pp.4–15, 2014]

'Risky business: When humor increases and decreases status' by T. Bradford Bitterly, Alison Wood Brooks and Maurice E. Schweitzer [*Journal of Personality and Social Psychology*, Vol. 112, No. 3, pp. 431–455, 2017]

'How humor in advertising works: A meta-analytic test of alternative models' by Martin Eisend [*Marketing Letters*, Vol. 22, No. 2, pp. 115–132, 2011]

'The Ostrich Effect: Selective Attention to Information' by Niklas Carlsson, George Loewenstein and Duane Seppi [*Journal of Risk and Uncertainty*, Vol. 38, No. 2, pp. 95–115, 2009]

Look Out: The Advertising Guide for a World That's Turning Inwards by Orlando Wood [2021]

Dumb Ways to Die by Melbourne Metro www.dumbwaystodie.com.

'Humor in Advertising: The Moderating Role of Prior Brand Evaluation' by Amitava Chattopadhyay and Kunal Basu [*Journal of Marketing Research*, Vol. 27, No. 4 pp. 466–476, 1990]

'Relationships among affective and cognitive factors in humor' by Frank Wicker, Irene Thorelli, William Barron and Marguerite Ponder [*Journal of Research in Personality*, Vol. 15, No. 3, pp. 359–370, 1981]

'Should I use humor in advertising?' by Millward Brown [2007]

16

THE PEAK-END
RULE

IT HAS BEEN a busy day. You've managed to get lots of work done, been out shopping and even had an eye test.

You mull over the day's events and your thoughts turn to the embarrassing faux pas at the client meeting. What was the name of that client who you failed to recognise? Was it Ann? Anna? Anya? Or Annabella?

You still can't quite remember. You curse your faulty memory.

YOUR PATCHY RECOLLECTION of a day's events is typical. Acute observers have long noted the quirks of memory. In *Mansfield Park* Jane Austen says:

There seems something more speakingly incomprehensible in the powers, the failures, the inequalities of memory, than in any other of our intelligences. The memory is sometimes so retentive, so serviceable, so obedient; at others, so bewildered and so weak; and at others again, so tyrannic, so beyond control!

Our brains don't have the capacity to store every moment. Instead, we capture a fraction of what happens to us. The author Milan Kundera reflects this tendency in his book *Immortality* when he says, "memory does not make films, it makes photographs". By that, he means that we remember snapshots of events, rather than their entirety.

Since our memory is selective, overall events can be remembered differently depending on which specific elements get lodged in our minds.

Helpfully, psychology provides guidance on the moments that stick. In this chapter I want to discuss one such theory: the 'peak-end rule'. This is the finding that we tend to remember the most (or least) enjoyable parts of an experience and the final moments.

> We tend to remember the most (or least) enjoyable parts of an experience and the final moments.

Some of the earliest evidence comes from a 2003 experiment by Donald Redelmeier, from the University of Toronto, and Daniel Kahneman, who at the time was based at Berkeley.

The pair ran a trial among colonoscopy patients. If you're unfamiliar with this operation, it involves a doctor inserting a flexible camera into your rectum to look for inflamed tissue or polyps. Pretty unpleasant.

The psychologists gave the volunteers handheld devices to record their pain levels every minute throughout the procedure. Later the patients gave two retrospective ratings for how unpleasant the operation was: one was given immediately afterwards, the other a month later.

Interestingly, the recollections didn't correspond well with the average level of pain experienced. Instead, the patients' memories were better predicted by two specific moments: the peak intensity of the pain and the discomfort felt in the final moments of the procedure.

So, how can you make painful colonoscopies work for you?

How can you apply this bias?

1. Focus on the moments that matter

The finding that some moments matter more than others is helpful as it guides us as to where to focus our efforts.

However, you might query the relevance of colonoscopies to your day job. Are the findings applicable to brands?

That's a fair objection, but the peak-end rule has been shown to exist in many situations. Perhaps most relevantly, three psychologists at Dartmouth College, Amy Do, Alexander Rupert and George Wolford, ran an experiment in 2008 to see if the peak-end applied to commercial situations.

Do and her team organised a charity raffle – anyone who made a donation was in with a chance of winning some DVDs. Later, the researchers emailed 100 of the entrants to tell them they had won and asked them to pick which title they wanted from a predetermined selection.

Some people were shown a range of highly rated films, as judged by the review site Rotten Tomatoes (list A). Others were shown a selection of more mediocre titles (list B).

The participants were then asked, on a seven-point scale, how pleased they were with their DVD. Unsurprisingly, those who picked from the superior list were happier. The mean score of those given list A was 5.21, compared to just 2.57 for the others.

So far, so predictable.

But then came the clever bit. Half of the participants were offered a chance to pick an extra DVD but this time from the alternative list. So, now there were four groups. You can see the difference in their ratings in the table below:

Group	Description	Mean rating
A	One DVD from the best list	5.21
B+A	One DVD from each list (ending with a pick from the best list)	4.82
A+B	One DVD from each list (ending with a pick from mediocre list)	4.14
B	One DVD from the mediocre list	2.27

Source: adapted from Do, Rupert and Wolford (2008).

The results corroborate Kahneman and Redelmeier's finding about the power of endings. A comparison of the groups that selected two DVDs reveals that ratings improved if the best title was picked last. Even though participants in those groups received the same prizes, the order mattered – those who ended on a high were 16% happier with the outcome!

Intrigued by this research, in 2020 I designed a test to see if the peak-end rule affects ads. Working with Alex Maguire at Unruly, we began by trawling through ads that had been analysed using Affectiva's second-by-second facial coding. Their methodology provides a score for the ads based on the audience reactions.

We selected nine ads that had the same overall scores. However, we split them into three groups based on their second-by-second profile. The groups were:

- Consistent ads that had a flat score from start to finish.
- Spiky ads that had pronounced peaks and troughs in their ratings.
- Spiky-end ads that had a peak moment at the end.

Next, we recruited 579 people to watch the ads. A week later we questioned them about their recall. There was a clear pattern. In terms of ad recall, 23% of people could remember the consistent ads, 31% the spiky ads and 33% the spiky-end ads.

We saw a similar pattern with brand recall: 10% of people could correctly remember the right brand for the consistent ads, 32% the spiky ads and 21% the spiky-end ads.

On both metrics, ads that harnessed the peak-end rule were far more memorable.

Now you know about the peak-end rule, what should you do? There are three tactics to apply when thinking about brand experiences:

- Fill in the troughs (that's minimising the negative peak).
- Amplify the pinnacles (that's accentuating the positive peak).
- End on a high.

Let's discuss each of these tactics in detail.

2. Start by filling in the troughs

Of the three tactics, filling in the troughs is the priority. You need to identify the worst part of your experience and improve it wherever possible.

This is the most important step because people exhibit a negativity bias: negative information has a bigger influence on us than positive information of the same magnitude. This occurs for two reasons.

First, we're more likely to remember negative information. This is demonstrated by a 1991 experiment conducted by Felicia Pratto at Berkeley. She asked participants to read a list of 40 personality traits: 20 negatives and 20 positives. When they tried to recall as many traits as they could, they were twice as likely to remember the negatives as the positives.

Second, even accounting for greater memorability, we tend to give negative information more weight than the equivalent positive event. That finding is best shown by a 1966 study by Shel Feldman from the University of Pennsylvania. Feldman gave participants a description of a person and then asked them to rate the appeal of the fictitious subject.

Sometimes the participants saw a description with a positive trait, sometimes a negative trait and sometimes both. The overall ratings of the mixed review were repeatedly more negative than a simple average would suggest. The psychologist argued that this demonstrated that bad information carried more weight than good information.

Our negativity bias might have evolutionary roots. Roy Baumeister, a psychologist at Case Western Reserve University, argues that:

It is evolutionarily adaptive for bad to be stronger than good. We believe that throughout our evolutionary history, organisms that were better attuned to bad things would have been more likely to survive threats and, consequently, would have increased probability of passing along their genes.

So, the evidence is clear that you should prioritise filling in the troughs. But what does that look like in practice? Well, it'll vary with the specifics of your brand, but let's look at some examples to make it more concrete.

Let's start with Disney. If you've visited one of their parks, you'll know that queuing makes up a sizable chunk of your stay – a popular ride can have a wait of almost two hours. Disney has filled this trough by entertaining those in line. For example, those waiting for the *Dumbo* ride are given a pager which buzzes when it's their turn to start the ride. In the meantime, visitors can take their children to the Dumbo-themed soft play area, housed appropriately enough in a circus big top.

It's not just children who are entertained in Disney's queues. In the line for the *Haunted Mansion* five sculptures line the wall, each with a plaque outlining the grizzly cause of their death. Your task is to use the clues to guess who murdered them all.

Disney spends significant sums on entertaining queuers, but solutions don't have to be expensive. Sometimes it just takes a bit of lateral thinking.

A lovely example of such left-field thinking comes from a Houston airport in the early 2000s. The management were dismayed by the number of complaints from passengers waiting at the baggage carousel: by this point travellers were often at the end of their tether and the delay, which was on average about eight minutes, tested their patience.

The management's response was almost costless. They re-routed passengers after passport control, so the travellers had to walk further. About eight minutes further in fact. This meant that by the time they arrived at the carousel their bags were already there.

Even though the time they picked up their bags was the same, complaints plummeted. In the words of Alex Stone, who reported on the Houston redesign for the *New York Times*, "the experience of waiting is defined only partly by the objective length of the wait". What matters more is perception and an unoccupied wait feels far longer than an occupied one.

THE ILLUSION OF CHOICE

The examples of Disney and Houston airport show the value of prioritising troughs. Too many companies shy away from dealing with the unpleasant parts of their products. It's often more exciting for a marketer to amplify the highs. But the evidence suggests that's the wrong place to start.

3. Amplify the pinnacles

Only once you have tackled your troughs should you turn to the next step: amplifying the pinnacle.

Simple? Maybe – but how many brands apply this thinking? Most attempt to make marginal improvements to every aspect of the customer experience. But that spreads their efforts thinly and damns them to mediocrity. After all, it's prohibitively expensive to meaningfully improve everything.

So, instead focus on making one moment truly stand out.

Once again let's look at an example, this time the Magic Castle hotel, which features in Chip and Dan Heath's excellent book *The Power of Moments*.

The Magic Castle is ranked by Tripadvisor as one of the Top Ten hotels in Los Angeles. An impressive 93% of the 3,512 reviews rate it as 'very good' or 'excellent'. That's a higher proportion than the famous Four Seasons in Beverly Hills.

In many ways its success is surprising as the hotel is basic: dated décor, spartan suites and a small swimming pool. And it comes at quite a cost. I tried to book a single room with a month's notice.

The price? A far from magical £254 a night – in line with a Marriott.

But the hotel masterfully applies the peak-end rule. Rather than create a uniform experience it focuses on creating one or two outstanding moments. One such moment is the popsicle helpline.

Any time, day or night, you can pick up the old-fashioned red phone by the pool and dial the helpline. A man, replete with white gloves, promptly appears bearing a silver platter with a selection of free ice-lollies.

It's creating stand-out moments – rather than marginally improving everyday aspects – that generates great memories and, in turn, excellent reviews.

However, suggesting you amplify the pinnacle just raises more questions, in particular, what makes a great moment? One factor is surprise. Consider the Magic Castle hotel. If you have been to a hotel, you'll have a set of expectations about what your stay will be like. The Magic Castle contravenes those expectations in a positive way. That boosts memorability.

That's not conjecture. The importance of surprise is demonstrated by an experiment conducted by Vani Pariyadath and David Eagleman, two academics at the Baylor College of Medicine in Texas. In 2007 they showed 84 participants nine photographs which each flashed up for between 300 and 700 milliseconds. Eight were the same mundane image – a brown shoe, whereas one was surprising – an alarm clock.

The academics then asked the participants to judge how long the image had been shown for, compared to the preceding image. The key finding, which became known as the oddball effect, was that the surprising image was judged to have been shown for 12% longer than it actually was.

So, focus on building a pinnacle that challenges the expectations of your audience. What's your equivalent of the popsicle hotline?

4. End on a high

The final application of the peak end is the simplest: end on a high. Often the temptation with brands is to focus on making a great first impression. And while that is important, Redelmeier

THE ILLUSION OF CHOICE

and Kahnemans's work argues that in terms of memories it's more important to end on a high.

So, who does that well?

Once again Disney are masters at applying this idea at their theme parks. When you start queuing for a ride there's a digital display that estimates how long you'll be waiting. However, TouringPlan, a site that helps visitors get the most from their trip to Disney's theme parks, compared two million displayed and actual wait times. They have found a consistent pattern of overestimation. Disney repeatedly warns you that a queue will take longer than it actually does.

At first glance that's surprising: why would a brand exaggerate their problems? But if you consider their actions in light of the peak-end rule, it makes sense. By overestimating the queue length, the experience ends on a high: the irritation of a 45-minute queue is minimised if you were expecting a 50-minute wait.

Disney isn't the only brand that applies the peak-end rule. Flat Iron has their own twist on the concept. If you haven't heard of them, Flat Iron is a chain of ten steak restaurants that was founded in London in 2012 by Charlie Carroll.

After you've paid the bill, the waiter gives you a pair of miniature ornamental steak knives and tells you to hand them in to the staff at the door when you leave. When you do, you're rewarded with a salted caramel ice cream cone in return. A surprise that ensures the dining experience ends on a high.

But perhaps my favourite example of a powerful ending is from the cinematic tradition of a post-credit sequence, sometimes known as the stinger. This is the practice of enticing the audience to stay to watch the credits with the reward of a bonus piece of content.

The trend started slowly with Bond films, which from 1963's *From Russia with Love* onwards included a short message placed after the main action, saying "James Bond will return in...".

However, in the late 1970s filmmakers began to fully exploit the idea when they added a more light-hearted touch. In 1979 *The Muppet Movie* broke the fourth wall by having the characters reappearing and talking to the audience. Most memorably with Animal yelling to those hanging around in the cinema "Go home!! Go home!! Bye!"

In the 1980s a number of films, such as the *Cannonball Run* franchise, started running outtakes after the main film. The inclusion of bloopers was wonderfully parodied by Pixar Animation, who ran them – of course without having any genuine ones – after films such as *A Bug's Life* (1998), *Toy Story 2* (1999) and *Toy Story 3* (2010).

Perhaps the best example comes from the 1978 John Landis film, *Animal House*. At the end of the main film there was a section showing what happened next to the characters. One of the characters, Babs, was shown getting a job as a tour guide at Universal Studios. Then after the credits rolled a static ad appeared saying "When in Hollywood visit Universal Studios (Ask for Babs)". Until 1989, anyone who took advantage of this cryptic suggestion was rewarded with a discount.

The peak-end rule helps marketers as it gives us guidance on where to focus. You need to make sure you fill in the troughs, then amplify the pinnacles and finally make sure you end on a high.

I'm afraid the peak-end rule is our final experiment. Hopefully, the tales of colonoscopies and bloopers has meant that we ended on a high.

REFERENCES

'Memories of colonoscopy: a randomised trial' by Donald Redelmeier, Joel Katz and Daniel Kahneman [*Pain*, Vol. 104, No. 1, pp. 187–194, 2003]

'When more pain is preferred to less: Adding a better end' by Donald Redelmeier, Barbara Fredrickson and Charles Schreiber [*Psychological Science*, Vol. 4, No. 6, pp. 401–405, 1993]

'Evaluations of pleasurable experiences: The peak–end rule' by Amy Do, Alexander Rupert and George Wolford [*Psychonomic Bulletin & Review*, Vol. 15, No. 1, pp. 96–98, 2008]

'The attention-grabbing power of negative social information' by Felicia Pratto and Oliver John [*Journal of Personality and Social Psychology*, Vol. 61, No. 3, pp. 380–391, 1991]

'Motivational aspects of attitudinal elements and their place in cognitive interaction' by Shel Feldman. In S. Feldman (Ed.), *Cognitive consistency*. [New York: Academic Press, pp. 75–108, 1966]

'Bad is Stronger than Good' by Roy Baumeister, Ellen Bratslavsky, Catrin Finkenauer and Kathleen Vohs [*Review of General Psychology*, Vol. 5, No. 4, pp. 323–27, 2001]

The Power of Moments by Chip Heath and Dan Heath [2017]

'The Effect of Predictability on Subjective Duration' by Vani Pariyadath and David Eagleman [*PLoS ONE*, Vol. 2, No. 27, e1264, 2007]

CONCLUSION

THE ROYAL SOCIETY is Britain's pre-eminent scientific academy. Founded in London in 1660, it has enabled some of the greatest advances in knowledge throughout history. It published Newton's *Principia* and funded James Cook's trip to Tahiti to monitor the transit of Venus, which helped size the solar system.

But what's most interesting to us is its guiding principle, encapsulated in its motto:

Nullius in verba

Or, in English, take nobody's word.

At the heart of this institution, and indeed science itself, is the idea that authority alone is not enough to establish a truth.

It's one of the reasons I love behavioural science. Nothing is argued from authority alone. No one, even illustrious Nobel Laureates like Kahneman and Thaler, is taken on their word. Everything must be proved experimentally.

This focus on evidence means the findings we've been discussing are robust. That's an improvement on much marketing or business theory, which is often based on the beauty of an argument rather than a cold analysis of data.

Surely, it's better to base our decision on the robust foundations of behavioural science rather than speculation?

But robust insights are only valuable if you use them. So, take these insights into human nature that behavioural science catalogues and apply them to your marketing. It'll make your efforts to change the behaviour of others more effective.

We've covered an awful lot of experiments in the last couple of hundred pages. Hopefully they have provoked plenty of ideas for practical changes to your marketing.

However, even though we have covered 16½ broad ideas (and if you pick up *The Choice Factory* there are another 25 insights worthy of consideration) that still leaves much we haven't discussed.

Psychology studies date back to the 1890s. Since then there have been thousands upon thousands of experiments. The ones we have analysed make up a tiny proportion of the entire body of work.

So, please don't stop here. There's plenty more to discover. And to help you on your way I have eight book recommendations that you might like to turn to next...

RECOMMENDED READING

The Choice Factory by Richard Shotton [2018]

Perhaps I'm a little biased about this one. But if you enjoyed *The Illusion of Choice* then you'll probably appreciate *The Choice Factory*. In it I identify 25 behavioural biases that influence consumer decisions. For each of the biases I look at the academic evidence, experiments that I've run to show those studies are relevant commercially and, most importantly, the practical applications.

Alchemy by Rory Sutherland [2019]

Anything written by Rory Sutherland is worth reading. He has a uniquely fertile imagination, so even when discussing biases and experiments you might be familiar with, he'll surprise you with a left-field interpretation. If you prefer listening to reading, then he's a regular podcast guest.

Blindsight: The (Mostly) Hidden Ways Marketing Reshapes Our Brains by Matt Johnson and Prince Ghuman [2020]

Most books on behavioural science are written with a generalist reader in mind. This book is particularly interesting as it demonstrates the marketing significance of the topic.

How to Change *by*
Katy Milkman [2021]

Milkman is one of the foremost authorities on behaviour change. We discussed her work at the beginning of the book in terms of the fresh start effect.

Atomic Habits: An Easy & Proven
Way to Build Good Habits & Break
Bad Ones *by James Clear [2018]*

The single best book on habits. A wonderful blend of stories and studies which are valuable from both a professional and personal perspective. You can read many of his articles here: jamesclear.com/articles

Priceless *by William Poundstone [2010]*

I recommended this book at the back of *The Choice Factory* so apologies if adding it here feels like a bit of a cheat. But there's no other book on pricing that comes anywhere close to being as interesting and informative as Poundstone's book.

The Power of Moments: Why Certain
Experiences Have Extraordinary Impact
by Chip and Dan Heath [2017]

The Heath brothers have written a remarkable collection of books about the business application of ideas from psychology. Their earlier book, *Make it Stick*, investigated how to make your communications more memorable. It's an excellent book but I've recommended *The Power of Moments* as it's equally good, has less overlap with other books on psychology and I drew on it more heavily while writing *The Illusion of Choice*.

Everybody Lies: Big Data, New Data, and What the Internet Can Tell Us About Who We Really Are *by Seth Stephens-Davidowitz [2017]*

My favourite book of 2017. The book covers one of the main themes of behavioural science: that you can't rely on what people say motivates them to understand what actually does. But rather than just point out the dangers of surveys and focus groups, he proposes the analysis of search volumes as an alternative tactic.

ACKNOWLEDGEMENTS

The research for this book draws on work conducted over the last five years. In that time I've been assisted by many people. For the first year, Lauren Leak-Smith provided me with invaluable assistance. Since then, Joanna Stanley has worked tirelessly to identify studies to include and has analysed their key findings. Without her this book wouldn't have been possible.

The actual writing of the book hasn't taken quite so long but others have been equally helpful. Nick Fletcher, Craig Pearce and Chris Parker have provided exemplary editorial and design advice.

Finally, my family.

My children, Anna and Tom, have provided plenty of encouragement. And, most of all my wife, Jane, who is a fantastic copywriter, has helped with the tone of voice of the book and general direction.

INDEX

ABOUT THE AUTHOR

Richard Shotton specialises in applying behavioural science to marketing. He has worked in the field for 22 years and in 2018 founded the consultancy Astroten. Astroten helps brands such as Google, Meta, BrewDog and Barclays use behavioural science to solve their marketing challenges.

Richard is the author of *The Choice Factory* which identifies 25 behavioural biases which can be used to solve business challenges. *The Choice Factory* is now available in 12 languages and was winner of best sales and marketing book at the Business Book Awards.

In 2021 Richard was made an honorary fellow of the IPA and an associate of the Moller Institute, Churchill College, Cambridge University.

He tweets about the latest social psychology findings from the handle @rshotton.

CPSIA information can be obtained
at www.ICGtesting.com
Printed in the USA
JSHW032128270123
36809JS00006BA/6

9 780857 199744